LEVANT
المشرق

The sun rises from the east over
the lands of the historic Levant
— modern day Palestine, Syria,
Lebanon, Israel and Jordan.
The shared culinary traditions
of this region offer opportunities
for reinvention, inspiration and
conviviality. It is in this spirit
that this book takes its title.

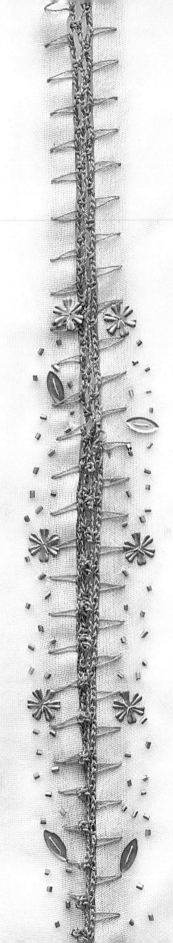

LEVANT

New Middle Eastern Flavours

RAWIA BISHARA

WITH SARAH ZORN

PHOTOGRAPHS BY CON POULOS

KYLE BOOKS

CONTENTS

INTRODUCTION 9
PANTRY INGREDIENTS 13

BREAKFAST & BAKED GOODS · 17

COOL & WARM MEZZE · 37

SALADS & SIDES · 65

MAIN DISHES · 101
vegetarian · 103
meats · 132
seafood · 159

SWEETS · 175

BEVERAGES · 195

SAUCES, MARINADES & GLAZES · 207

INDEX 220
ACKNOWLEDGEMENTS 224

RECICES

DIETARY SYMBOLS

V - Vegetarian

VE - Vegan

GF - Gluten Free

N - Contains Nuts

BREAKFAST & BAKED GOODS

Four Cheese Frittata V · 19

Green Tomato Shakshuka V, GF · 20

Smashed Broad Beans with Avocado V, VE, GF · 22

Spring Asparagus Casserole V, GF · 23

Falafel Scotch Eggs V · 25

Spinach & Cheese Pastry Triangles V · 26

Rolled Mushroom Omelettes V, GF · 27

Everything Grilled Cheese Sandwiches V · 28

Gluten-Free Flatbread V, GF · 31

Basic Flatbread V · 33

Manakeesh

    Labneh, Red Onion & Kalamata Olive V · 34

    Halloumi, Green Za'atar & Sumac V · 34

COOL & WARM MEZZE

Cocktail Mushrooms with Three Cheeses V · 39

Quinoa-Stuffed Tomatoes V, GF, N · 40

Roasted Beetroot Houmous V, VE, GF, N · 42

Butternut Squash Houmous V, VE, GF, N · 42

Avocado Houmous V, VE, GF, N · 44

Roasted Pepper Houmous V, VE, GF, N · 44

Dukkah-Spiced Lentil Spread · 46

Spicy Lamb Egg Rolls N · 47

Syrian String Cheese V, GF · 49

Oil-Cured Chilles with Walnut Stuffing V, VE, GF, N · 53

Filet Steak Shawarma Sliders · 57

Green Za'atar Puffs V · 58

Kibbeh Cups N · 60

Halloumi Bites with Hot Tomato Jam V · 63

SALADS & SIDES

Coriander Salata V, VE, GF · 67

Fennel, Pomegranate & Sage Salad V, GF · 68

Bitter Greens with Sweet Tahini Dressing V, VE, GF, N · 70

Watermelon, Halloumi & Za'atar Salad V, GF · 73

Freekeh Salad with Spring Vegetables V · 74

Crunchy Kohlrabi and Jicama Slaw V, VE, GF, N · 77

Autumn Fattoush V, VE · 78

Quinoa Tabouleh V, VE, GF · 81

Grilled Sweetcorn Salad V, VE, GF · 82

Artichoke & Tomato Sauté with Pesto V, VE, GF, N · 83

Quinoa Pilaf with Roasted Vegetables V, GF · 84

Warm Orzo with Artichoke Hearts V, N · 86

Aubergine Hash with Tomatoes V, VE, GF · 87

Tangy Roasted Root Vegetables with Goat's Cheese V, GF · 89

Pan-Roasted Potatoes & Leeks with Teklai V, VE, GF · 90

Lebanese Spicy Pan-Fried Potatoes V, VE, GF · 91

Squash with Chickpeas in Minted Yogurt V, VE, GF · 92

Homemade Yogurt V, GF · 94

Spicy Skillet-Crusted Rice V, VE, GF · 95

Coriander Green Beans with Toasted Almonds V, VE, GF, N · 97

Sautéed Hearts of Courgette V, VE, GF · 98

MAIN DISHES

VEGETARIAN

Portobello Shawarma V, VE · 103

An Excuse for Kibbeh V, VE, N · 104

Stuffed Aubergine over Toasted Pita V, VE · 109

Cauliflower Tahini Tagine V, VE, GF, N · 111

Freekeh-Stuffed Turnips with Tamarind Sauce V, VE · 112

Fresh Broad Beans with Spiced Yogurt Sauce V, VE, GF · 115

Egyptian-Style Lentil & Noodle Pilaf V, VE · 116

Crispy Cauliflower Steaks V, GF · 119

Jerusalem Artichoke & Sage Sauté V, VE, GF · 120

Chickpea Soup with Baby Onions V, VE, GF · 121

Baked Pumpkin Kibbeh V, VE, N · 122

Rawia's Sweet & Sour Soup V, VE, GF · 125

Jerusalem Artichoke & Sweet Potato Soup: V, VE, GF · 126

Freekeh and Shiitake Soup V, VE · 129

Butternut Squash Napoleons V, GF · 130

MEAT

Tahini Chicken Curry **GF** · 132

Five Onion Chicken **GF** · 133

Harissa Baked Chicken **GF** · 135

Baked Chicken Kibbeh **N** · 136

Chicken & Aubergine Rollatini · 138

Bahraini Chicken with Rice **GF** · 141

Tanoreen Spiced Poussins **GF, N** · 143

Braised Beef & Mushrooms with Almond Teklai **N** · 145

Aleppo-Style Kibbeh Stew with Carrots · 146

Lamb-Stuffed Potatoes in Tamarind Sauce **GF, N** · 149

Sweet & Sour Beef Rolls **GF** · 151

Beef Stew with Quince **GF** · 154

Braised Oxtails with Green Olives **GF** · 155

Holiday Roasted Leg of Lamb **GF** · 156

SEAFOOD

Pan-Roasted Salmon with Salsa Khadra **GF, N** · 159

Walnut-Crusted Fish Fillets **N** · 160

Grilled Fish Kabobs **GF** · 162

Moroccan-Style Stuffed Sardines · 165

Aunt Um Sami's Baked Fish Kibbeh **N** · 166

Grilled Sesame Prawns **GF, N** · 168

Christmas Seafood Artichokes **N** · 171

SWEETS

Olive Oil, Butternut Squash & Carrot Cake **V, N** · 177

Chocolate Baklava **V, N** · 179

Jam & Tahini Squares **V, N** · 180

Pistachio-Stuffed Chocolate-Dipped Fruit **V, GF, N** · 181

Honey-Cured Aubergine **V, N** · 182

Swirled Molasses Pudding · 184

Triple Almond Cake **V, GF, N** · 187

Caraway Pudding · 188

Crispy Walnut-Stuffed Crescents · 189

Layered Custard and Nut Crumble **V, N** · 190

Butter Cookie Sandwiches **V** · 193

BEVERAGES

Iced Hibiscus Tea **V, GF** · 197

Rose Water Lemonade **V, VE, GF** · 197

Tamarind Cooler **V, GF** · 198

Ginger Orangeade **V, VE, GF** · 198

Sun-Dried Apricot Nectar **V, VE, GF** · 199

Golden Turmeric Milk **V, GF** · 202

Anise Tea **V, VE, GF** · 202

Cinnamon Tea **V, GF, N** · 203

Sage and Fennel Tea **V, GF** · 203

Sipping Custard with Orange Blossom **V, GF, N** · 204

White Coffee **V, VE, GF** · 204

SAUCES, MARINADES & GLAZES

All-Purpose Tahini Sauce **V, VE, GF, N** · 209

Tahini Yogurt Sauce **V, GF, N** · 209

Tahini Pomegranate Sauce **V, VE, GF, N** · 209

Tarator **V, VE, GF, N** · 210

Forty Cloves of Garlic Sauce **V, GF** · 211

Harissa **V, VE, GF** · 212

Hot Pepper Paste **V, VE, GF** · 212

Spicy Tomato Sauce **V, VE, GF** · 213

Cilantro-Basil Pesto **V, GF, N** · 216

Teklai **V, VE, GF** · 217

Tanoreen Peanut Sauce **V, VE, N** · 218

Pomegranate-Tamarind Glaze **V, VE, GF** · 219

Seafood Marinade **V, VE, GF** · 219

WHAT'S OLD IS NEW AGAIN

MY FIRST BOOK, *Olives, Lemons & Za'atar,* was defined by my most cherished food memories of growing up in the Middle East. This book is a continuation of that journey through the olive groves and into the city, from my mother's kitchen and into my own.

Cooking is about history and tradition, but to remain vibrant, a cuisine must also evolve. And my hope is that with this book we can do that together.

When I moved to the United States, Middle Eastern (and, specifically, Palestinian) fare was largely absent from the culinary landscape. But since I had grown up surrounded by exquisite, deeply flavourful food that I knew everyone would love, I promised myself that one day I would find a way to share it on a greater scale. The seed was planted.

I started off small, as I hadn't gone to culinary school or taken a cooking class in my life, but learned how to cook first in my mother's kitchen and then for my own family, when I moved to the United States. I started throwing dinner parties using traditional ingredients and techniques I had learned back home. But as time passed and I travelled, explored and visited different kinds of restaurants, I grew more adventurous. I began to use Middle Eastern ingredients in innovative ways and experimented with ingredients outside the Middle Eastern pantry.

By the time I sent my children off to university, I was ready to open Tanoreen. The first incarnation of my dream was a humble, ten-table shopfront in Bay Ridge, Brooklyn, where I toiled away preparing the genuine Palestinian home cooking I grew up with. I knew it was a big risk, but I told myself, make it about the food, cook with love and it will shine right through. And here we are, two decades later.

Writing my first book was a walk down memory lane. I shared what has been in the world of Middle Eastern cooking, with only a few hints of what it would become. Now I can confidently say that this is what it became. While my second book adheres to the general landscape of the Levantine kitchen, it also veers sharply away from labels and boundaries, indulging in some exhilarating culinary rebellion with Mexican poblano chillies, Japanese breadcrumbs, as well as quinoa, Jerusalem artichokes, ginger, basil and a whole lot more. This is Middle Eastern cooking that has caught up with time, without compromising authenticity or cohesion. As far as Arabic food goes, it is healthier, easier to make and more important, tastier!

This evolution continued to take shape when I moved from the cramped shopfront space into full-fledged restaurant quarters with a much bigger kitchen and staff one street away. Just as significantly, I took my daughter, Jumana, on as my business partner; the two of us share a symbiotic love not only of good food, but pride in being Palestinian women running a successful and thriving restaurant in one of the biggest food cities in the world.

New York City — a famed melting pot of cultures — has left an indelible imprint on Tanoreen, and the restaurant is constantly informed by the travels and experiences of family and friends as well. My daughter brought the national dish of Egypt, *koshari,* to my attention after she returned from finishing her master's degree in Cairo. My version is in the book on page 116. My son — who currently calls California home — introduced me to some of our newcomer ingredients including Jerusalem artichokes and quinoa. My close friend Yolanda exposed me to the Halabi cuisine of Syria, which is illustrated in my Aleppo-Style Kibbeh Stew with Carrots (page 146). I even re-imagine Japanese beef *negimaki* in the form of my Sweet & Sour Beef Rolls (page 151), equally inspired by the roast my mother would make for us as children. In place of the sticky, often cloying teriyaki sauce used in restaurants, I swap pomegranate molasses and red wine.

I explore Asian, Indian, South American and Italian flavours and aromas without ever abandoning my Middle Eastern beginnings. On any given day at Tanoreen, you'll find a tahini-thickened curry dish sharing tables with vegan Portobello Shawarma (page 103) and decadent, gluten-free Triple Almond Cake (page 187) served alongside cups of traditional orange blossom–perfumed White Coffee (page 204).

In previous decades, Middle Eastern home cooking relied on vegetables and grains to offset the monetary stress of feeding a big family, but nowadays it has become more meat-centric. Here, while I offer choices from the land, air and sea, my recipes are outnumbered by vegetarian, vegan and gluten-free dishes that more closely adhere to the classic Mediterranean diet. Look for Butternut Squash Napoleons (page 130) anchored by swipes of Roasted Beetroot Houmous (page 43), Scotch eggs surrounded by falafel (page 25), kibbeh created from pumpkin and spinach (page 122), and a main course-worthy Kohlrabi & Jicama Slaw (page 77).

They say that salt makes your food taste ten per cent better. I say, cook what you like, take risks in the kitchen, switch out ingredients, be courageous with your palate, and prepare your food with love and your meal will come out one hundred per cent better.

I'm all about taking what you know and building upon that. Tamarind, for instance, is a relatively new discovery for me, one that I've used to add depth and texture to dishes and to impart a welcome tartness that I have even used in place of my beloved lemon. My Spicy Tomato Sauce (page 213) will be recognisable to Middle Easterners as a base for

stewing string beans or okra, but it is an equally excellent stand-in for *arrabiata* pasta. Do you love *shakshuka* but aren't feeling the red? Make it green, as I have here, using Mexican tomatillos, Arabic squash, and poblano chillies. Or if you don't especially like squash, use artichoke hearts instead. As long as it's green, it works!

My point is to feel free to break the rules. Nothing makes me happier than to walk through the dining room at Tanoreen and be eagerly stopped by a guest who can't wait to confess that she had never liked vegetables or a certain type of meat, but was converted when she tried my version. I can't help but feel proud and it confirms that I made the right decision all those years ago.

A few years ago, I fell ill, and a long recovery left me with plenty of time to think about how best to contribute to my own well-being. My clear-as-day conclusion was to utilise restorative foods, both at Tanoreen and in this second book. I began to incorporate nutritional powerhouses such as turmeric, extra virgin olive oil, nut flours, salmon, quinoa and freekeh into my cooking and found ways to tuck fresh vegetables and herbs into anything and everything.

I am not one to make grandiose claims that food can heal all ailments. Still, I believe that small changes and substitutions can contribute to a healthier lifestyle without sacrificing one bit of flavour and enjoyment. Nothing is lost and everything is gained through feel-good, taste-great dishes like Quinoa Tabouleh (page 81), Salmon with Salsa Khadra (page 159), and olive oil-moistened Butternut Squash & Carrot Cake (page 177).

The effect that food can have is incredible, not just on our physical well-being, but on our emotional state as well. For me it's about togetherness and family, conviviality and conversation. I would love for you to be able to peek inside my Monday (day-off) dinners at home, when everyone gathers to eat. Wine flows, while we work together to construct a charcuterie board chock-full of *sujok* (Armenian sausage), halloumi and *kashkaval* cheeses, olives, pickles and toasted bread. My son cooks seafood perfumed with saffron and herbs and my husband barbecues, while my daughter and I help prep the meal. Add in loving friends to partake in our joint efforts for a simply unforgettable eating experience.

I don't want food to just taste good. I want it to taste fantastic! And I want you to savour the care and effort put into making it so you can have experiences similar to the ones I regularly enjoy. I want you to use food to form new memories.

Opening Tanoreen pushed me to think about cooking in a different way. It called on me to venture beyond the traditional and expected to shape an entirely new cuisine, one that is sophisticated but still relates to the classic Middle Eastern kitchen. This book represents my mind-opening, life-changing journey, and it is my deepest wish that you enjoy these dishes as much as I enjoyed creating them.

Life is truly beautiful over a good meal.

PREVIOUS PAGE: Enjoying coffee with my daughter, Jumana.
THIS PAGE, TOP: At Tanoreen restaurant.
BOTTOM: A lesson together on Syrian String Cheese (page 49).

SOME OF MY FAVOURITE PANTRY INGREDIENTS

BASMATI RICE: *Basmati* means 'my smile' in Arabic. It forms the traditional base of my all-purpose Rice & Vermicelli Pilaf (page 140); it's all you'll need to turn any dish into a meal.

BLACK PEPPER: As essential as salt (I'd even argue more so), black pepper should really *always* be freshly ground. A mill and some peppercorns are absolutely worth the investment.

BULGAR WHEAT: Though I've started to swap it in classic preparations like *shulbato* (page 84) and tabouleh, bulgar (cracked wheat berries) remains fundamental in kibbeh.

Tip: Bulgar is graded accorded to texture from ultra-fine to very coarse. Check labels to make sure you purchase the right one for your recipe.

CHICKPEAS: Keep a stash of chickpeas in your cupboard at all times, whether dried or tinned. Useful for so much more than houmous (try my Squash wih Chickpeas in Minted Yogurt, page 92). They're an incredibly thrifty way to add bulk to your meal, plus they provide a hefty dose of protein and fibre.

Tip: If you're using tinned beans in a recipe, always drain away the liquid and heat the beans in a pan with a little olive oil first; this revives them and takes away the tinned taste.

DRIED CHILLIES: In addition to boiling and puréeing chillies to make Hot Pepper Paste (page 212), they

OPPOSITE, FROM TOP: Sesame seeds, za'atar, sumac.

can be ground into a powder to season raw or baked kibbeh.

Tip: While I still order chillies from overseas (such as the fruity Aleppo chilli), I also readily use chillies more easily found near me, such as anchos and guajillos from Mexican markets.

FREEKEH: The world has begun to catch on to what the Middle East has known for years. This ancient grain — harvested when it's young and green — is practically unmatched in its nutritional benefits. And it's got a nutty, grassy flavour that can't be beat.

GROUND ALMONDS: A delicious gluten-free alternative increasingly found in supermarkets, natural food stores, and gourmet shops.

Tip: Ground almonds can be expensive, but making your own is very easy to do. Simply pulverise whole almonds in a food processor to a fine, sandy texture, stopping before they turn into a paste. It's not the end of the world, however, if you go too far, as almond paste (marzipan) is a wonderful thing too.

HOT CHILLI OIL: This fiery infused oil can be used both for cooking and as a condiment; try drizzling it on top of a bowl of good houmous.

Tip: I used to buy bottles of hot chilli oil from Asian markets, but I've found it's just as easy to make my own. Especially at the end of summer, when I have tons of serrano chillies turning red on the vine in my garden! Just cut a narrow slit in a whole chilli (any variety will do), drop it into a bottle or jar, top with 1.5 litres of olive oil and seal tightly. Let sit for a few days to infuse.

HOT PEPPER PASTE: If you ask me, there are few recipes that don't benefit from a dab of hot pepper paste. It takes minutes to make your own (page 212), or make sure to buy a brand that's little more than a blend of chillies and water without an excess of flavourings or salt.

KIBBEH SPICES: What was once a fusion of lamb and bulgar wheat — the national dish of many Middle Eastern countries, from Lebanon to Syria to Palestine — has been expanded to incorporate chicken, fish and even vegetables. But the spice mix that also defines kibbeh (including allspice, coriander and cloves) has largely remained the same. You can purchase a ready-to-use blend online.

LENTILS: Quicker to cook than most dried beans, they come in a surprising variety, from mild and tender brown lentils to firm and peppery green and sweet silky red.

LIMU: As much as I love lemons, I must confess to a soft spot for these dried Persian limes. Because they're dehydrated and preserved, an intriguing smoky note cuts through the intense, lusty acidity. And once procured from a Middle Eastern market (or purchased online), they'll keep forever in your pantry.

Tip: Release limu's smoky, earthy flavours by poking holes in them before dropping them in stock or stews (like Bahraini Chicken with Rice, page 141), or grind them into powder and use them as you would a dried spice.

MASTIC: This piney resin taken from the mastic tree (and used as a flavouring for toothpaste and bubble-gum) is also a star ingredient in desserts, adding a fresh, fragrant sweetness to puddings, ice cream and cakes.

NUTS: Almonds, walnuts, pistachios and pignolis are used with abandon in the Middle East (and in my kitchen), finding their way into everything from stuffing for kibbeh to a crust for fish fillets to a base for pastries and even a garnish for beverages.

OLIVE OIL: Extra virgin olive oil, to be exact — why bother with anything else? The only other oil you need is vegetable or corn oil for high-heat frying.

ORANGE BLOSSOM WATER AND ROSE WATER: While frequently combined in recipes, they're actually quite different. The former is intensely fruity, while the latter is powerfully floral — and both are intoxicating when (sparingly) stirred into drinks and desserts.

PANKO: Any kind of breadcrumbs will do in a pinch, but I adore Japanese panko, which forms a fluffier, crispier crust on deep-fried foods like Crispy Cauliflower Steak (page 119) and makes for an airy filling for Cocktail Mushrooms with Three Cheeses (page 39).

Tip: Take your panko for a spin in the food processor if you prefer a smaller crumb.

POMEGRANATE MOLASSES AND GRAPE MOLASSES: While pomegranate molasses is sourer and grape molasses is sweeter, both are the pride of a Middle Eastern pantry. As you'll see in recipes in this book, I use pomegranate molasses often in sauces, glazes and stews. Like honey, grape molasses can stand in for sugar as a sweetener.

QUINOA: As healthy as freekeh (it's also a complete protein), quinoa is one of my new favourite grains and it also happens to be gluten-free. Since it absorbs flavours wonderfully, it's taken the place of bulgar in many of my otherwise traditional salads.

SUMAC: The dried, powdered berries of a flowering bush, sumac is not supposed to be salty or cherry red. True sumac should have a pure lemon flavour and an almost purple colour (the darker the better!), which means the farmers have waited for the fruit to get really ripe before harvesting it. If you think you may have purchased what I call 'cheated sumac' (sumac with other ingredients mixed in), just make sure to taste your food before adding any extra salt.

TAHINI: I could probably devote an entire book to this miraculous ingredient. A pure paste made by grinding down raw or toasted sesame seeds, it's the only superb sauce, spread, dressing or condiment you will ever need on its own. But combined with just one or two other items, it becomes something truly out of this world.

Tip: How's this for a breezy dessert? Tahini plus carob molasses. Just think of it as an Arabic version of peanut butter and jelly!

TAMARIND: Growing up in Galilee, I associated these sticky, fruity pods with two things — a refreshing drink sold on the streets of Jerusalem and a dish of lamb and rice–stuffed turnips and purple carrots bathed in sweet and sour sauce (which became the base of my Freekeh-Stuffed Turnips with Tamarind Sauce; page 112). But when I moved to New York City, I learned how popular tamarind is throughout the world and was encouraged to expand my personal repertoire and seek out its signature tang in soups, sauces, roasted meats and more.

Tip: Look for jars of tamarind paste concentrate, which comes ready to use. Other forms include whole pods, boxes of pulp and bottles of syrup, which are very dark and exceedingly sour.

TANOREEN SPICE MIX: You'll be able to divide many of our ingredient lists in half if you have to hand a single jar of Tanoreen Spices, a nine-item powerhouse of rosebuds, cardamom, cinnamon, allspice, black pepper, ginger, coriander, cumin and cloves. Not only will you be able to replicate my dishes exactly, your food will taste precisely like my mom's — and that's a wonderful thing. It's available from the restaurant.

VINEGAR: In the old days, people used to rely on salt for preservation. But taking advantage of vinegar — especially white or apple cider — allows you to pickle anything and cut back on the sodium content while you're at it.

ZA'ATAR: While I'll mention it in the spice section later on, I have to give lip service one more time to the magnificent herb, za'atar. Wild thyme or oregano mixed with sumac, salt and sesame seeds — it's the ultimate topping (not to mention the namesake of my first book).

BREAKFAST
&
BAKED
GOODS

THE FAMILY GATHERS, A NEW DAY BEGINS

Truth be told, I waffle (pun intended) about whether I am a breakfast person or not. I tend to be improvisational about what I eat in the morning; sometimes a full meal is in order, and other times a good cup of coffee with a digestive biscuit or some fruit will suffice.

That said, I am fascinated by breakfast traditions around the world, as they are reflections of a culture's past as well as its present. People are serious about how they choose to break the nighttime fast, and Palestinians are especially passionate about their practices, with supporting small plates playing as important a role as the main event.

Here are a few basic rules of the Palestinian breakfast table: it should always contain wedges of tomato and slices of cucumber, a dish of olives without a doubt, surely a bowl of za'atar and extra virgin olive oil, absolutely a slab of cheese or *labneh* (strained yogurt), and lots of toasted Arabic bread. Consider it a Middle Eastern continental breakfast of sorts, and after that, the possibilities are endless.

The following suggestions for fleshing out your morning feast are alternately hearty (as represented by the not just one, two, or three, but Four Cheese Frittata; page 19), tangy and light (Sumashed Broad Beans with Avocado, page 22), and just different enough to provoke a slight tilt of the head, à la my Mexican-inspired Green Tomato Shakshuka (page 20).

FOUR CHEESE FRITTATA

While this extra-cheesy vegetable frittata makes an excellent brunch item (especially since the vegetable mixture can be sautéed the night before, in order to save time), it's delicious served at room temperature. Which means you can make it over the weekend and enjoy leftovers for a quick lunch on Monday. It's also great cut into small wedges like a Spanish tortilla and served at cocktail parties. **MAKES 8–10 SERVINGS**

120ml olive oil, plus more for the pan

2 shallots, diced

3 leeks, white parts only, thinly sliced (about 120g)

2 bunches asparagus, woody ends removed, cut into 2.5cm pieces

100g fresh spinach

1 long hot or poblano chilli, diced (optional)

12 extra large eggs

½ teaspoon baking powder

½ teaspoon bicarbonate of soda

½ teaspoon freshly grated nutmeg

1 teaspoon freshly ground black pepper

Sea salt

125g finely chopped feta cheese

115g finely chopped halloumi cheese

115g shredded kashkaval cheese (see page 50)

225g cottage cheese or ricotta cheese

Fresh cut cucumbers and tomatoes, for serving

Preheat the oven to 180°C/gas mark 4.

In a large frying pan, heat 60ml of the oil over a medium heat. Add the shallots and cook for about 3 minutes, until starting to soften. Add the leeks and cook for an additional 3 minutes. Add the asparagus, spinach and chilli and cook for another 3 minutes, or until the spinach is wilted, then turn off the heat. Drain the mixture into a colander to remove excess moisture. Let cool. (You can make the recipe up to this point a day ahead; cover and refrigerate until ready to use.)

In a large bowl, beat the eggs, then beat in the baking powder and bicarbonate of soda. Add the nutmeg and black pepper and season with salt. Add all four cheeses and the vegetable mixture and stir to combine.

Coat the bottom and sides of a deep 30 x 45cm baking dish with oil. Pour the egg mixture into it and drizzle the remaining 60ml oil on top. Place in the oven for 10 minutes, then reduce the oven temperature to 135°C/gas mark 1 and bake for another 25 minutes, or until when you poke the middle of the pan, the eggs are cooked through and not runny.

Remove from the oven and let cool for a few minutes, then cut into squares. Serve with fresh cut cucumbers and tomatoes alongside.

GREEN TOMATO SHAKSHUKA

At the summer's end, I'm always left with big, green tomatoes in my garden that haven't fully ripened. One time, I thought to make shakshuka – otherwise known as 'eggs in purgatory' – with them. They lent the dish a vibrant, lemony flavour that I just adored.

Of course, one can't find green tomatoes year-round. So I thought, why not use tart tomatillos instead? They ended up tasting even better than the green tomatoes, and I've never gone back. **MAKES 4–8 SERVINGS**

150ml olive oil, plus 2 tablespoons

4 shallots, thinly sliced

7 cloves garlic, diced

2 poblano chillies, thinly sliced

2 long hot chillies (or 1 small green pepper for milder taste), thinly sliced

7 small Arabic squash (a type of bulbous, green-striped summer squash) or 2 large courgettes, cut into 1.25cm-thick slices

6 large or 10 small tomatillos, husks removed (or 4 large green tomatoes), washed and cut into 1.25cm-thick slices

2 medium yellow tomatoes, cut in 1.25cm-thick slices, or 320g cherry tomatoes, sliced in half

2 tablespoons tomato purée

1 tablespoon Hot Pepper Paste (page 212)

Juice of 1 lemon

1 teaspoon ground cumin

1 teaspoon sea salt

1 teaspoon freshly ground black pepper

8 large eggs

Grated halloumi cheese, for serving (optional)

Preheat the oven to 180°C/gas mark 4.

In a large, nonstick ovenproof frying pan, heat 4 tablespoons of the oil over a medium heat. Add the shallots and cook for about 5 minutes, until starting to soften. Add the garlic, poblanos, long hot chillies and squash and cook until just tender, about 8 minutes. Remove to a plate.

Add 2 tablespoons more of the oil to the pan and add half of the tomatillos. Do not stir. Cook until the tomatillos just begin to colour on one side, about 3 minutes, then flip them. When the second side begins to colour, about 3 minutes more, remove the tomatillos to a plate. Repeat with the remaining tomatillos, adding more oil to the pan if it looks dry. Leave the second batch of tomatillos in the pan. Top with the reserved squash mixture, followed by the reserved tomatillos and the yellow tomatoes.

In a small bowl, whisk together the tomato purée, hot pepper paste, lemon juice, cumin, salt and black pepper and spread the mixture evenly over the vegetables. Cover the pan and cook over a low heat for 5–8 minutes, until all the ingredients have softened. If the mixture starts looking dry, add up to 120ml water.

Uncover the pan and evenly drizzle the remaining 4 tablespoons oil over the vegetables. Using a spoon, make shallow indentations in the mixture, and carefully crack the eggs over the top. Place the frying pan (uncovered) in the oven and bake until the whites are set and the yellows are cooked to your liking, 5–8 minutes for runny or 10–12 minutes for firm.

Sprinkle the top with grated cheese, if using. Switch on the grill and place under the heat until just melted. Bring to the table and serve immediately, straight from the pan.

SMASHED BROAD BEANS
WITH AVOCADO

When I prepare 'my father's broad beans', I'm talking about classic stewed broad beans with lemon, garlic, olive oil and a bit of tahini mixed in. That's always how he made *ful mudammas*. But some people are allergic to sesame nowadays, so I needed to find a substitute. And I did, in rich and smooth avocado, which provides the perfect texture and taste to offset the sturdy beans. Then I took it a step further by adding red onion, poblanos, coriander and jalapeños, which essentially created an Arabic spin on Mexican guacamole. Combining cultures is what we do best in New York! **MAKES 4–6 SERVINGS**

3 limes

2 Hass avocados

2 x 300g tins broad beans, drained

165ml olive oil

5–6 cloves garlic, finely chopped

1 teaspoon ground cumin

½ teaspoon sea salt

40g chopped fresh coriander

1 poblano chilli, finely chopped

½ red onion, finely chopped

4 rings of pickled jalapeño, plus 6 tablespoons of the pickling brine (see Note)

Tortilla chips or Arabic bread (such as pitta or Flatbread, page 33), for serving'

Roll the limes to get their juices flowing, then juice them. Chop 1½ of the avocados, thinly slice the remaining avocado half, and place them in separate bowls. Cover the avocado with the juice of 1 lime to keep them from browning.

In a large saucepan, combine the broad beans with 6 tablespoons of the oil and heat over a very low heat until just warmed through. Add the garlic, cumin, salt, the remaining lime juice and the remaining 5 tablespoons oil. Add the chopped avocado and mash until the mixture is thoroughly combined with a creamy texture. Turn the heat off and add half of the coriander, half of the chilli, half of the onion and all of the pickled jalapeños and brine and mix very well.

Spoon onto a serving plate and garnish with the remaining coriander, chilli and onion and the sliced avocado. Serve with Arabic bread or tortilla chips.

NOTE: To make the dish less spicy, omit the pickled jalapeños and use 90ml fresh lemon juice in place of the pickling brine.

Star Ingredient
When people talk about 'good fats', buttery and fruity avocados are one of them. It turns out sesame seeds are too!

SPRING ASPARAGUS CASSEROLE

This is inspired by my father's favourite breakfast when I was growing up. He would forage wild asparagus from the forest by our house between March and June, when the stalks were quite tender with a purplish hue. He prepared them with fresh eggs from the chicken farmer down the road. You can't get more farm-to-table than that.

My version at the restaurant is filled with fragrant fresh herbs, melty cheese and robust poblanos, which makes the dish substantial, yet delicate. Served with sliced tomato and perhaps some olives and cucumber, this casserole transports me straight back to my childhood. **MAKES 8–10 SERVINGS**

120ml olive oil, plus more for the pan

2 large shallots, chopped

2 medium poblanos, deseeded and diced

1 large garlic clove, chopped

400g asparagus tips cut into 2.5cm pieces

25g chopped fresh coriander

15g chopped fresh basil

2 tablespoons chopped fresh sage

Pinch of freshly grated nutmeg

½ teaspoon freshly ground white or black pepper

Sea salt

12 large eggs

225g ricotta cheese or cottage cheese

115g shredded mild melting cheese (I like *kashkaval* or smoked Gouda)

4 plum tomatoes, sliced into rounds

Olives and sliced cucumber, for serving

Preheat the oven to 180°C/gas mark 4. Grease a large rectangular, square or round baking dish.

Heat the oil in a deep frying pan over a medium heat. Add the shallots and cook for about 3 minutes, until starting to soften. Add the chilli and cook for 3–5 minutes. Add the garlic and cook for 1½–2 minutes. Add the asparagus, coriander, basil and sage and cook until the asparagus is crisp-tender. Add the nutmeg and white pepper and season with salt. Remove from the heat and cool.

In a large bowl, beat the eggs, then beat in the ricotta cheese until well incorporated. Fold in the vegetable mixture. Pour into the prepared baking dish, top with the shredded cheese and tomato slices, and bake until the eggs are set (not runny) when pierced with a fork, and the casserole is golden brown on top, about 30 minutes. Slice into squares or wedges and serve warm or at room temperature, with olives and cucumber slices alongside.

FALAFEL SCOTCH EGGS

Growing up, I remember there were breakfast carts in Jerusalem that sold only three items: boiled eggs, falafel and sesame bread. Yes, falafel is eaten for breakfast in the Middle East, and often!

One Easter, I had boiled more eggs than I could colour. So I thought back to those Jerusalem breakfasts I loved so much and decided to find a way to marry those flavours together. I encased the freshly boiled eggs in my classic falafel mix (entirely unaware of the Scotch tradition of doing the same with sausage) and threw them in the fryer. Believe it or not, they were as attractive as they were delicious. Once sliced open, the green, herb-flecked insides look terrific against the ivory egg white and yellow yolk. Serve with a simple green salad or your choice of sauce (see pages 209–221). **MAKES 8 EGGS**

8 large eggs

½ yellow onion, roughly chopped

3 cloves garlic

15g coarsely chopped fresh flat-leaf parsley

10g coarsely chopped fresh coriander

½ jalapeño chilli (or chilli of your choice), coarsely chopped

450g dried chickpeas, soaked overnight with water to cover by a few centimetres

1 tablespoon freshly ground black pepper

1½ tablespoons ground coriander

1 tablespoon ground cumin

1½ teaspoons sea salt

½ teaspoon bicarbonate of soda

Corn or vegetable oil, for frying

Cook the eggs: Place the eggs in large saucepan and add cold water to cover. Turn the heat to high and bring to the boil. Remove from the heat, cover, and let stand for 3 minutes. Carefully drain, then fill the pan with ice water to cool the eggs. Gently crack the shells and carefully peel them under cold running water. Set aside.

Make the falafel: Finely chop the onion in a food processor. With the motor running, add the garlic through the feed tube, then add the parsley, coriander, and chilli. Stop the motor, add the chickpeas and process until when you squeeze a portion of the mixture in your palm, it comes together easily like dough but isn't pasty. If it is too firm and crumbly, add a bit of water. If it is too soft, add a bit of flour or breadcrumbs.

Transfer the mixture to a bowl and add the black pepper, coriander, cumin, salt and bicarbonate of soda. Using your hands or a rubber spatula, gently incorporate the spices while tossing the mixture as you would a salad.

Fill a medium saucepan or deep-fat fryer with oil (deep enough to submerge your eggs) and heat it to 185˚C, or until when you drop a small piece of the falafel mixture in the oil it crisps quickly and floats to the surface.

Scoop out 8 palm-size portions of the falafel mixture. Flatten them into an oval shape and place an egg on top of each. Moisten your hands with water and gently mould the falafel mixture around the eggs until they are evenly coated.

Working in batches if needed, gently drop the eggs into the oil. Fry until golden brown all over, 4–5 minutes. Using a slotted spoon, remove the eggs to kitchen paper to drain.

NOTE: If you'd prefer to bake your eggs instead of frying them, lightly coat the outsides with olive oil, place on baking trays, and cook in a 200°C/gas mark 6 oven for 35 minutes.

SPINACH & CHEESE PASTRY TRIANGLES

BOUREKAS

Israel's Ministry of Education used to send schoolteachers on a type of vacation or sabbatical – called *betta'havrah* – as a gift. On one such trip, my mother was sent to a small resort near Tel Aviv, where she was exposed to an entirely different, largely European cuisine. Which meant that when she came home, she was chock-full of culinary inspiration.

One significant discovery for her was puff pastry. She would wrap it around an apple filling and bake it, resulting in warm and sweet apples and crisp, buttery dough. At the time, it was a genuinely new taste sensation. She also used puff pastry in savoury applications, as I've done here. These spinach and cheese pockets are as good for breakfast and brunch as they are on an afternoon picnic.

By the way, I'm aware that making puff pastry from scratch is a lot of work. So while I applaud your efforts if you feel up to the challenge, I'd strongly advise simply buying it from the chilled or frozen food section in the supermarket. **MAKES 24 PASTRIES**

450g feta cheese, crumbled

450g farmer's cheese or cottage cheese

450g fresh baby spinach, chopped, steamed and squeezed dry, or chopped frozen spinach, defrosted and squeezed dry

120ml olive oil

2 shallots, finely chopped

1 red onion, finely chopped

Sea salt

Chilli flakes

2 x 215g puff pastry sheets, defrosted

2 eggs, beaten with a splash of water or milk

Preheat the oven to 200°C/gas mark 6.

In a large bowl, combine the cheeses, spinach, oil, shallots and red onion and season with salt and chilli flakes.

For individual pockets, divide the two sheets of puff pastry into 12 squares each. Alternatively, you can leave the sheets whole. Place your squares or whole sheets on two large baking pans.

For individual pastry pockets, dab spoonfuls of filling in the centre of each square and fold over to make triangles. Crimp the edges with a fork to close. If leaving whole, evenly divide the filling and place in the centre of each of the two sheets of puff pastry. Fold the short sides of dough as far as they'll go over the filling, and roll the long sides over so that the filling is encased in dough.

Brush the rolls or triangles with egg wash and bake until golden, about 20 minutes. Serve warm.

ROLLED MUSHROOM OMELETTES

During the week, we would always have a quick breakfast before heading to work or school – labneh, za'atar, pickles, jam, bread, maybe a boiled egg. But on my mum's days off from teaching, she would frequently make us *iijeh*, or omelette, scrambled with a bit of parsley, mint, spring onions, or whatever fresh herb or vegetable she was growing behind the house. Since she was a true artist when it came to food, her iijeh was extra special, with a slice of melted cheese tucked into the centre as well.

On his day off, my dad liked to collect fresh mushrooms from the woods, which he would sauté with spices and a bit of lemon and they tasted just like meat. Needless to say, my father was not a traditionalist – when most men would steer clear of the kitchen, he jumped right in and helped my mother cook on a consistent basis. That's why my perfect iijeh draws on childhood food memories from both my mother and father. There's so much you end up learning and incorporating into your own life just by watching and imitating your parents – especially when they were as good as mine were. **MAKES 4 SERVINGS**

MUSHROOMS

4 tablespoons olive oil

2 shallots, thinly sliced

½ long hot, jalapeño, or poblano chilli, seeded and thinly sliced

2 cloves garlic, sliced

¼ teaspoon ground allspice

½ teaspoon freshly ground black pepper

½ teaspoon sea salt, or to taste

2 tablespoons chopped fresh sage

2 tablespoons chopped fresh coriander

450g mixed mushrooms (I like shiitakes and baby portobellos), sliced

Juice of ½ lemon

IIJEH

8 large eggs

1 tablespoon chopped fresh mint

½ teaspoon freshly ground black pepper

Dash of sea salt

½ teaspoon ground turmeric

1 tablespoon olive oil

4 slices *kashkaval* cheese (see page 50), plus more for garnish

Make the mushrooms: In a large frying pan, heat the oil over a medium heat. Add the shallots and cook for 6–8 minutes, until golden brown. Add the chilli and garlic and cook for another 3–5 minutes, until tender. Add the allspice, black pepper, salt, sage, coriander and mushrooms. Increase the heat to high and cook, stirring often, until the mushrooms are tender. Turn off the heat and add the lemon juice. Let cool. You can prepare this a day ahead and refrigerate until you're ready to finish the dish.

Make the iijeh: In a large bowl, beat the eggs with the mint, black pepper, salt and turmeric. Heat the oil in a medium pan over a medium heat. Pour one-quarter of the egg mixture into the pan. When it begins to set and colour on the bottom, carefully flip it over. Place a generous scoop of the mushroom mixture down the middle and top with a slice of cheese. Cook until the second side is set, then fold over both sides and remove to a heatproof dish. Repeat to make three more iijeh. Spoon the remaining mushroom mixture over the omelettes and garnish with a few more slices of cheese. Place under the grill until the cheese is just melted. Serve immediately.

EVERYTHING GRILLED CHEESE SANDWICHES

When I say grilled cheese, I mean grilled cheese, in that every last component of these sandwiches is grilled. And while I list specific ingredients here, I invite you to use this recipe as more of a jumping-off point. In fact, you can even go the sweet route by keeping the cheese and avocado, spreading honey on the bread, and tucking in slices of watermelon (grilled rind is the best!).

Surprised by the suggestion? To me, this is the most natural combination in the world. I was first introduced to avocado by my father, who would slice the buttery fruits in half, remove the stones, fill the centres with honey and serve them to us with a spoon. **MAKES 2 SANDWICHES**

2 pitta pockets

225g halloumi cheese (1 block), cut through the centre into two thinner blocks

4 slices slightly under-ripe, best quality tomato, such as heirloom, beefsteak or similar

1 ripe but firm avocado, peeled, stoned, and flesh cut into 4 thick slices

1 small cucumber, peeled and cut lengthways into 4 thick slices

2 firm 5cm-thick slices watermelon, cut from near the rind

2 slices red onion (optional)

1 jalapeño or long hot chilli (optional)

Olive oil, for brushing

Sea salt and freshly ground black pepper

2 pitta pockets

Chopped fresh coriander, for serving

Lightly brush the cheese, tomato, avocado, cucumber, watermelon, onion slices and jalapeño, if using, with oil and sprinkle with salt and pepper.

Place everything except the pittas on a lightly greased grill or griddle pan, heated until hot but not smoking, and cook until grill marks develop, about 2 minutes on each side (the cheese may take slightly longer). Transfer grilled items to a plate. Brush the pittas with oil and place on the grill until warmed through but not crisp, about 1 minute on each side.

Slice about 1.25cm off of the top of each pitta to expose the opening inside. Slice the chilli, if using, into rounds and fill each pitta with 1 block of cheese, 2 tomato slices, 2 avocado slices, 2 cucumber slices, 1 slice watermelon, 1 onion slice and half of the chilli rounds, if using. Top with a handful of fresh coriander. Cut each sandwich in half lengthways and serve.

NOTE: Instead of using shop-bought pitta, make a batch of my flatbread dough (page 33, or try the gluten-free version on page 31), lightly oil both sides, cook it directly on the grill, about 3 minutes per side, then roll your sandwiches instead of stuffing them. You could also use pizza dough. The cheese can be omitted if you prefer to go vegan.

THE MEANING OF MANAKEESH

If cooking is an act of love, making manakeesh is pure romance. How else would you define someone taking time out of a busy schedule to bake you sheets of delicious, pizza-like flatbread?

Back when I was young, manakeesh was prepared daily in most homes in the Middle East. Since it was costly to buy it at the market, families on budgets would work their ovens with homemade dough to help stretch every meal.

Take into account large household sizes (I was one of five; my husband was one of eight) and you'll see that breadmaking is a labour of love, indeed, for the baker in charge (generally Middle Eastern mothers).

The most common manakeesh varieties were za'atar and olive oil and red pepper and sesame, as they were affordable, readily available toppings that delivered on flavour. They were served with fresh tomato or cucumber – rather splendid in their simplicity, as warm bread always is.

But that was then and this is now. And while my sense of food tradition is very firmly rooted in the authentic food I grew up with, I also enjoy a bit of risk and adventure at my restaurant. Which is why I set out to modernise manakeesh both honouring the years of my mother's studious, selfless baking and exciting the palates of contemporary diners.

Once I met the challenge of creating an ideal flatbread dough, I decided to stretch the boundaries further. After endless tweaking, I arrived at the holy grail – entirely gluten-free manakeesh that mimics the original perfectly.

It's important to get the balance of the chewiness and crispiness just right. Because as much as I enjoy a crusty, crunchy pizza, I don't want the bread to taste like a cracker. The same goes for toppings: their allure lies in their slightly contradictory qualities. Take my halloumi pie, for instance. The cheese is salty and squeaky, the pomegranate seeds are supple and sweet, the green za'atar is almost combatively herbaceous, and the sumac is scarlet and lemony. The cooling, creamy labneh version is equally distinct, amplified with rings of biting red onion and briny, mysteriously dusky kalamata olives. Finally, the sujok and cheese version features robust and garlicky Armenian sausage in a sea of melty, gooey chilli cheddar cheese.

As with many of the recipes and methods I have included in this book, versatility and self-expression are key. So as much as manakeesh is considered street food, it can also be breakfast, a late-night supper, and a cocktail party appetiser all in one. You can substitute pizza dough if you are in a rush and need to get things done in half the time. Because – in cooking, at least – love is expressed through intent, not through hours of effort.

GLUTEN-FREE FLATBREAD

MAKES 12 LARGE OR 24 SMALL FLATBREADS

1 teaspoon sugar

2 teaspoons active dried yeast

480g gluten-free flour

100g ground almonds

4 large egg whites, beaten

1 tablespoon sea salt

4 tablespoons milk powder

1 tablespoon mahlab (optional; see below)

180ml olive oil

In a small bowl, dissolve the sugar and yeast in 120ml warm water and set aside for 5 minutes, or until the mixture is foamy.

Add the gluten-free flour, ground almonds, egg whites, salt, milk powder, mahlab, if using, oil, dissolved yeast and 240ml additional water to the bowl of a stand mixer fixed with the dough hook (or a large mixing bowl, if combining by hand). If using a machine, mix on low until the ingredients are just combined, and increase to medium. Mix by machine or hand for at least 5 minutes, or until the dough pulls away from the sides of the bowl, adding flour as needed if too wet, or water if too dry. You should have a springy but still slightly sticky dough.

Oil a large bowl and add the dough. Cover with clingfilm or a moistened tea towel and leave for about 1 hour, until the dough is doubled in size.

While the dough is rising, preheat the oven to 180°C/gas mark 4. Lightly grease a baking tray.

Lightly oil your hands and divide the dough into 12 or 24 equal-size balls. Let them rest on a flat surface until slightly expanded, 10–15 minutes.

Sprinkle a work surface with flour and roll the dough balls to about 1.25cm thickness. Place on the prepared baking tray (in batches if needed) and bake for 15–20 minutes, until golden. Enjoy as is, or with toppings (see page 34).

Mahlab

This precious spice is made from the powdered seeds of a type of sour cherry. And yes, when I say precious, I also mean expensive. So while it's a traditional addition to baked goods and sweet breads (adored for its nuanced, bitter almond flavour), you have my permission to omit mahlab, especially if it would keep you from making your own manakeesh.

BASIC FLATBREAD

MAKES 12 LARGE OR 24 SMALL FLATBREADS

1 teaspoon sugar

2 tablespoons active dried yeast

800g plain flour (or 520g plain flour plus
    260g wholemeal flour), plus more
    as needed

1 tablespoon sea salt

1 tablespoon mahlab (optional, see page 31)

240ml olive oil, plus more for greasing

200g low fat natural yogurt (not Greek), homemade
    (page 94) or shop-bought

In a small bowl, dissolve the sugar and yeast in 120ml warm water and set aside for 5 minutes, or until the mixture is foamy.

Add the flour, salt, mahlab, if using, oil, yogurt, dissolved yeast and 240ml additional water to the bowl of a stand mixer fixed with the dough hook (or a large mixing bowl, if combining by hand). If using a machine, start on low until the ingredients are just combined, and increase to medium. Mix by machine or hand for at least 5 minutes, or until the dough pulls away from the sides of the bowl, adding flour as needed if too wet or water if too dry. You should have a springy but still slightly sticky dough.

Oil a large bowl and add the dough. Cover and leave for about 1 hour, until the dough is doubled in size.

While the dough is rising, preheat the oven to 180°C/gas mark 4. Lightly grease a baking tray.

Lightly oil your hands and divide the dough into 12 or 24 equal-size balls. Let them rest on a flat surface until slightly expanded, 10 to 15 minutes.

Sprinkle a work surface with flour and roll the dough balls to 1.25cm thickness. Place on the prepared baking tray (in batches if needed) and bake for 15–20 minutes, until golden. Enjoy as is, or with desired toppings (such as Labneh, Red Onion & Kalamata Olives or Halloumi, Green Za'atar & Sumac, see page 34).

NOTE: The dough can be tightly wrapped in clingfilm and chilled for a few hours or overnight, or even frozen to bake later, although the texture won't be quite the same.

TOP: Roll the dough balls out to 1.25cm thickness; you can use a cutter (approximately 15cm in diameter) to cut out the dough if you'd like uniform circles, or you can simply roll out to a more rustic shape. **BOTTOM:** Use your fingers to press the centre of the dough circles slightly to create a small ridge around the edge (this will help to keep the topping intact); you may now pre-bake the plain bread as is then add substantial toppings such as those on the following page, or as shown here you may wish to spread a simpler topping (such as equal parts za'atar and olive oil) on the dough circles then bake.

MANAKEESH

The following two recipes each make enough to top four manakeesh. If you would like to bake an entire batch of the dough recipes (on pages 31 and 33), then you will need to double or triple the amounts of these toppings accordingly. Alternatively, you can work with just a portion of the dough at a time, and store the rest in the refrigerator or freezer for later use.

LABNEH, RED ONIONS & KALAMATA OLIVES

MAKES 4 MANAKEESH

8–10 tablespoons labneh

1 red onion, very finely chopped

120ml olive oil

Pinch of freshly ground black pepper

Pinch of chilli flakes or cayenne pepper (optional)

4 pre-baked flatbreads (can also use ready-made pide, pitta or naan)

50g stoned kalamata olives, sliced

Preheat the oven to 200°C/gas mark 6. In a small bowl, whisk the labneh and onion together with a fork. Whisk in the oil. Add the black pepper and chilli flakes, if using. Spread the labneh evenly over each piece of bread. Dot the tops with the olives and place in the oven for a few minutes, until sizzling.

HALLOUMI, GREEN ZA'ATAR & SUMAC

MAKES 4 MANAKEESH

450g halloumi cheese (2 blocks), or other Arabic cheese

25g coarsely chopped fresh green za'atar (see page 59)

225g pomegranate seeds

2 tablespoons sumac

120ml olive oil

4 plum tomatoes, sliced

4 pre-baked flatbreads (can also use ready-made pide, pita, or naan)

Preheat the oven to 200°C/gas mark 6. Grate two-thirds of the cheese. Cut the remaining third into long, thin slices. In a bowl, combine the grated cheese with the za'atar, pomegranate seeds, sumac and olive oil. Spread 1 of the sliced tomatoes out on each of the flatbreads. Top evenly with the grated cheese mixture. Using the remaining sliced cheese, arrange 4 slices on top of each flatbread in a star shape. Bake in the oven until the tomato is tender and the cheese is melted.

Sujok is a dry Armenian sausage that is robustly spiced and garlicky with a pronounced umami flavour. The harder it is, the better. I prepared it for quite some time as an appetiser, sautéed with chillies and lemon, before it dawned on me that it belonged on a flatbread (we generally used bread to sop up the spicy sauce I served with the sausage). My ideal accompaniments are fresh tomatoes and pepper Jack or chilli Cheddar (Arabic cheeses tend not to melt as well), but you can also use mozzarella or Cheddar. Just please, no processed cheese! Finish with a sprinkling of fresh basil or oregano and serve hot.

COOL & WARM MEZZE

MAKING WAVES WITH SMALL PLATES

So what, exactly, is mezze? It's about talking and relaxing, having a bite and a drink. The goal is not to fill up, but to satiate your senses as much as your stomach with a variety of flavours and textures. It's a little of this and a piece of that. It's slow and patient eating, passing plates and clinking glasses. Mezze is a mood and a good one at that.

Mezze is also the term we use to describe a style of eating consisting of several small plates eaten in advance of the main meal. The foundation of the spread traditionally is pickles and olives, warm bread, houmous, baba ghanoush, labneh and tabouleh. From there, it progresses to warm staples like falafel and kibbeh, stuffed grape leaves, and meat or spinach pies. Of course, there's much more you can add, but you will almost always find these items on the table.

However, after twenty years of serving world-beloved recipes in constant rotation, I thought it was time to shake things up. I decided to marry classic ingredients in unexpected combinations and introduce some decidedly non-Middle Eastern additions to the mix as well. A great example of this is makdous; baby aubergine stuffed with chilli paste and walnuts. I replaced the aubergine with poblanos and jalapeños (much more common in the Mexican kitchen) for crunch and heat and to change up something tried and true. The recipe is on page 109. The same goes for cauliflower steak, which has made a huge splash at the restaurant. The initial inspiration was from my mother (which is true of so much of my cooking), who would fry florets to a deep golden brown and top them with tahini. I slices the cauliflower into thick steaks instead and coated them in panko breadcrumbs before frying them until crispy. The result? A dish that's equally at home as mezze and main and a hit with both vegetarians and carnivores. Find the recipe on page 119.

COCKTAIL MUSHROOMS
WITH THREE CHEESES

We've all encountered dry and crusty stuffed mushrooms at a wedding or cocktail party, and more often than not, they're a letdown. But why should they be? Mushrooms are the perfect vessel for transporting a punch of pure flavour. Kashkaval cheese gives my stuffed mushrooms a creamy, Cheddar-like consistency, and briny halloumi's low moisture content helps keep the mushrooms from becoming an oozy mess. While it may be a bit retro to add sun-dried tomatoes to the mix, I love their concentrated sweetness and chewiness.

These garlicky, herbaceous hors d'oeuvres are the ultimate make-ahead appetiser or amuse bouche for a dinner party. Stuff them in the morning, throw them into the refrigerator, and forget them until just before your guests are due to arrive. **MAKES 20 MUSHROOMS**

STUFFING

115g shredded mozzarella cheese

115g shredded halloumi cheese

115g shredded kashkaval cheese (see page 50)

10 oil-packed sun-dried tomatoes, finely chopped

½ cup chopped fresh basil, or 1 tablespoon Coriander-Basil Pesto (page 216)

3 cloves garlic, chopped

Juice of 1 lemon, plus more for serving

2 large egg whites, beaten

6 heaped tablespoons toasted unseasoned bread-crumbs (I prefer panko)

2 tablespoons olive oil

½ teaspoon sea salt

½ teaspoon freshly ground black pepper

MUSHROOMS

20 large button mushrooms, stems removed and reserved

2 tablespoons olive oil

20g finely grated Parmesan cheese

480ml water or low-sodium chicken stock

Sea salt and freshly ground black pepper

Preheat the oven to 190°C/gas mark 5.

Make the stuffing: In a bowl, mix together all the stuffing ingredients until well combined.

Stuff the mushrooms: Spoon the stuffing into the mushroom caps and place them in a large baking dish. Drizzle the mushrooms with the oil and sprinkle with the Parmesan cheese. Pour the water around the mushrooms in the dish and season with salt and pepper. Add the reserved mushroom stems (they'll add nice flavour to the pan sauce).

Cover with aluminium foil and bake for 20 minutes. Uncover and bake for 3 minutes more, or until the tops are golden and the cheese is melted. Arrange the stuffed mushrooms on a serving plate and serve with a drizzle of the pan sauce and a bit of lemon squeezed over the top.

QUINOA-STUFFED TOMATOES

You'll find stuffed tomatoes at just about every steakhouse and Italian deli in New York, and they're all virtually identical – filled with a bit of cheese, a few herbs and lots of breadcrumbs. So I thought I'd put my own spin on them by adding lots of cheese, some za'atar, and just enough quinoa to hold everything together. I promise you won't miss the breadcrumbs! **MAKES 4–8 SERVINGS**

8 large tomatoes (I like vine tomatoes)

90g steamed quinoa

3 cloves garlic, roasted (see note below) and chopped

Sea salt and freshly ground black pepper

55g oil-packed sun-dried tomatoes, chopped

25g chopped fresh basil leaves

1 tablespoon Coriander-Basil Pesto (page 216) or shop-bought pesto

1 tablespoon dried za'atar

60ml olive oil

Juice of 1 lemon

115g shredded kashkaval cheese (see page 50)

115g finely chopped halloumi cheese

115g finely chopped Syrian String Cheese (page 49) or fresh mozzarella cheese

480ml chicken or vegetable stock

Chopped walnuts or almonds, for serving (optional)

Preheat the oven to 200°C/gas mark 6.

Slice 1.25cm from the tops of the fresh tomatoes and set the tops aside. Using a small spoon or knife, gently remove the seeds and set them aside.

Combine the quinoa with the garlic and season with salt and pepper. Add the sun-dried tomatoes, basil, pesto, za'atar, oil, lemon juice and cheeses and stir to combine. Stuff as much of the mixture as will fit into the tomatoes and replace their tops. (Any leftover stuffing can be enjoyed later, as a tasty side dish.)

Combine the reserved tomato seeds with the stock in a deep casserole dish, season with salt and stir to combine. Add the stuffed tomatoes in a single layer and cover with aluminium foil. Bake for 10 minutes, then reduce the oven temperature to 160°C/gas mark 3 and bake for an additional 10–15 minutes, until the tomatoes are very tender. Remove the foil and bake for 3–5 minutes more, until the tops are browned and bubbling. Serve with the pan sauce and nuts, if using.

NOTE: To roast garlic, cut 1.25cm from the top of a whole head to expose the cloves. Drizzle with olive oil and roast in a 200°C/gas mark 6 oven for 30–35 minutes, until the cloves are soft. Once the garlic is cool enough to handle, squeeze the head to pop out the cloves. Leftover roasted garlic has endless uses. It's incredible simply spread on toasted bread!

REDEFINING HOUMOUS

Houmous was a gateway dish of Middle Eastern cooking in America when I opened Tanoreen, and I watched it slowly weaving its way between food carts, falafel stands, and restaurants before it hit supermarket shelves.

I remember when my son and daughter called me, shocked to find houmous served with carrots at a cocktail party. That's how little Middle Eastern food was represented less than twenty years ago. Then I heard houmous mentioned on an episode of *Seinfeld*. I couldn't believe it. New Yorkers know houmous? But what's not to love about such a versatile food? It's traditionally eaten for breakfast, sometimes at lunch, and frequently in between meals, and it is always the first dish to kick off a mezze spread. In Galilee, there are houmous shops that serve it with chopped lamb and pine nuts, accompanied by warm bread and a jug of olive oil for drizzling. You eat it and go.

In Arabic, the word *houmous* literally translates to 'chickpea', which is why chickpeas have long remained the focus in our version of the dish. Smoothing it out with velvety tahini is entirely necessary, as is enlivening it with a bit of garlic, salt and lemon, but the star is the chickpea. Or was.

Somewhere along the line, houmous has come more to mean tahini dip, with or without chickpeas. In my own break from tradition, I decided to swap the chickpeas for beetroot, which lend an intense earthy character to the houmous, not to mention a conversation-stopping, deep magenta colour. I played with the flavour profile still further by adding pomegranate molasses and decided to put it on the menu for a couple of weeks to test it out. I couldn't believe the response. People started to call in advance to see if we had the beetroot houmous before committing to dining at the restaurant! It has been on the menu ever since.

From beetroot, I moved on to butternut squash, avocado and roasted pepper houmous, and every time I put them on the table — a rainbow of pale green, deep red, and faint orange — everyone smiles. Which means this is only the beginning. Now that we've received the blessing of our customers to move on from chickpeas, there's no shortage of new ideas for tahini dips!

ROASTED BEETROOT HOUMOUS

Whether using it as a dip, sandwich spread or salad dressing, you can do absolutely anything with this houmous except cook with it, as the high sugar content of the beetroot will cause it to burn in the oven. And you certainly don't want to sacrifice that gorgeous purple hue. **MAKES 950ML**

6 tablespoons olive oil

1 teaspoon freshly ground black pepper

2 teaspoons sea salt

1 tablespoon ground cumin

6 medium beetroot, peeled and sliced into 2cm thick rounds

115g tahini

3–4 cloves garlic, crushed

Juice of 3 lemons

4 tablespoons pomegranate molasses

Preheat the oven to 230°C/gas mark 8.

In a large bowl, whisk the oil with the pepper, 1 teaspoon of the salt, and the cumin. Thoroughly toss with the beetroot to coat. Place onto a baking tray, cover loosely with aluminium foil and roast for 45 minutes, or until fork tender. Set aside to cool.

In the bowl of a food processor, combine the tahini, garlic, lemon juice, pomegranate molasses, and the remaining 1 teaspoon salt and pulse until thoroughly incorporated. Continue to process for 2 minutes, gradually adding up to 60ml water, until the mixture reaches your desired consistency. Add the roasted beetroot and blend until semi-thick in consistency and pink in colour.

BUTTERNUT SQUASH HOUMOUS

This makes an incredible crust for a piece of fish. Just slather it on the bottom and top of your fillet – you don't even need to add oil – and stick it in the oven to roast. **MAKES 950ML**

2 large butternut squashes, peeled, sliced into 1.25cm thick rounds, and deseeded

Olive oil, for roasting

Sea salt and freshly ground black pepper

115g tahini

3 tablespoons tamarind concentrate, 120ml tamarind juice, or 4 tablespoons pomegranate molasses

120ml fresh lemon juice (about 2 large lemons)

3 cloves garlic, crushed

2 tablespoons chilli oil (optional)

Preheat the oven to 230°C/gas mark 8.

In a large bowl, lightly coat the butternut squash with oil and sprinkle with salt and pepper. Arrange in a single layer on a baking tray and roast until tender but not caramelised, 20–25 minutes, flipping halfway through. Allow the squash to cool to room temperature.

In the bowl of a food processor, combine the squash with the remaining ingredients and process until smooth. Taste and add more salt if needed.

AVOCADO HOUMOUS

The level of depth and creaminess tahini adds to already velvety avocado makes this dip a real winner. Consider it your new, go-to guacamole alternative – especially if you serve it with tortilla chips instead of pitta! **MAKES 950ML**

3 large Hass avocados, stoned, peeled, and coarsely chopped
1 poblano chilli, coarsely chopped (optional)
115g tahini
120ml fresh lemon juice
Zest and juice of 2 limes
3 cloves garlic, crushed
1½ teaspoons sea salt

Combine all the ingredients in a food processor and process until smooth.

ROASTED PEPPER HOUMOUS

Why relegate houmous to a dip? It may be a bit thick, but once it starts to melt and loosen in the oven, you'll find it also makes a spectacular sauce. Use this to marinate chicken and it will be the best bird you've ever tasted. **MAKES 950ML**

3 poblano chillies
3 green peppers
2 red peppers
Olive oil, for roasting
115g tahini
2 tablespoons pomegranate molasses
120ml fresh lemon juice
Juice of 2 limes
3 cloves garlic, crushed
1½ teaspoons sea salt

Lightly brush a grill or griddle pan with olive oil and heat to medium, or preheat the oven to 260°C/gas mark 10.

Lightly coat the chillies and peppers with oil and set them on the grill until blistered and tender, about 5 minutes, or roast in the oven for about 15 minutes. Place the chillies and peppers in a covered pan or paper bag for a few minutes to steam and loosen the skins. When cool enough to handle, peel away the skins and remove the seeds.

In a food processor, combine the chillies and peppers with the remaining ingredients and process until smooth.

DUKKAH-SPICED LENTIL SPREAD

There are many iterations of dukkah (which means 'to pound') throughout the Middle East, but its roots are in Egypt. It's an extremely flavourful mix of ground seeds, nuts and spices such as caraway, cumin, fennel, sesame seeds, hazelnuts, chickpeas, dried mint and much more, in endless combinations.

That said, growing up in Galilee, I did not have dukkah as part of my pantry. So I never even thought to use it, until a friend brought me a small bag from Gaza. When I tried it, I knew it was my long sought-after 'cure' for lentil dip; lending it a nutty, savoury, slightly sweet quality, so it didn't taste – quite frankly – so muddy and starchy. **MAKES 950ML**

350g dried brown lentils

180ml fresh lemon juice

180ml olive oil

1 tablespoon dill seeds

1 tablespoon chopped fresh dill, plus fronds for garnish

4 cloves garlic

1 long hot chilli of your choice, deseeded and sliced, or 1 tablespoon Hot Pepper Paste (page 212)

1 tablespoon ground cumin

1 tablespoon sea salt

½ teaspoon freshly ground black pepper

1 teaspoon chilli flakes

Toasted pitta chips, crackers, or vegetable crudités, for serving

In a large saucepan, bring 960ml water to the boil. Add the lentils and boil for 15–20 minutes, until tender. Drain and put the lentils into a food processor. Add the lemon juice and 120ml of the oil and process until smooth. Transfer to a bowl.

Using a pestle and mortar or the food processor (clean it out first), combine the dill seeds, fresh dill, garlic, chilli, cumin, salt, black pepper and chilli flakes and grind into a paste. Add the paste to the lentil purée and mix well to incorporate.

Spread the houmous onto a flat plate. Make an indentation in the middle and fill it with the remaining 60ml oil. Garnish with dill fronds and serve as a dip with toasted pitta chips, crackers or vegetable crudités. (It also makes a terrific spread for sandwiches.)

NOTE: Quicker to cook than most dried beans, lentils come in a surprising variety, from mild and tender brown lentils, to firm and peppery green and sweet, silky red.

SPICY LAMB EGG ROLLS

Living and cooking in New York City, it's hard not to get inspired by the various food cultures around you, especially when there's a Chinese restaurant located right next door. So I borrowed the idea of an egg roll and married it with a Palestinian meat pie (and made it a little spicier so it would stand up to all that dough) for a self-contained snack that's bound to be the talk of your next party. **MAKES 12 EGG ROLLS**

120ml olive oil

3 shallots, chopped

3 cloves garlic, diced

2 long hot chillies or another chilli of your choice

10g chopped fresh coriander

½ teaspoon freshly ground black pepper

1½ tablespoons Tanoreen Spice Mix
   or
   1 tablespoon ground allspice
   ½ teaspoon ground cumin
   ½ teaspoon ground coriander
   Pinch of cinnamon
   Pinch of freshly grated nutmeg

900g lean minced lamb (or very finely chopped lamb)

1 tomato, peeled and very finely chopped

2 tablespoons pomegranate molasses or 120ml fresh lemon juice

Sea salt

40g toasted flaked almonds (optional)

65g pine nuts (optional)

2 x 240–250g puff pastry sheets, defrosted, or 12 egg roll or spring roll wrappers

Vegetable oil, for frying

Tahini Pomegranate Hot Sauce (page 209), Tanoreen Peanut Sauce (page 218), or yogurt, for dipping

Heat the olive oil in a large sauté pan over a medium heat. Add the shallots and cook for about 4 minutes, until starting to soften. Add the garlic and chilli and cook until the garlic is golden, about 2 minutes. Add the coriander, black pepper and Tanoreen Spices and cook for 1 minute more. Add the lamb and tomato and cook until the meat is cooked through, 5–7 minutes. Add the pomegranate molasses, season with salt, add the almonds and pine nuts, if using, and stir to combine. Remove from the heat and let the mixture cool to room temperature.

If you are using puff pastry, cut each sheet into 6 equal squares. Angle the puff pastry squares or the egg roll wrappers towards you so they look like diamonds. Place a heaped spoonful of meat near the corner closest to you, and fold that corner of dough up over the mixture. Fold the left and right corners over the mixture, and finish tightly rolling up the dough like a cigar, until you reach the far corner.

Fill a pan or deep-fat fryer with enough vegetable oil to submerge the egg rolls. Heat the oil until hot but not smoking. Add the egg rolls in batches, and cook until golden on all sides, turning with a spatula, about 4 minutes. Alternatively, you can place the egg rolls on baking trays and cook in a 200°C/gas mark 6 oven for 15 minutes until golden.

Serve with Tahini Pomegranate Hot Sauce, Tanoreen Peanut Sauce, or yogurt for dipping.

SYRIAN STRING CHEESE

This is a recipe for authentic Syrian string cheese, which is nothing like the individually wrapped, rubbery sticks sold in supermarkets. This type of cheese is something I had never eaten until I moved to America.

One day – years before I opened the restaurant – I walked into a Syrian-owned speciality food shop in Brooklyn and spotted an older woman behind the counter stretching out long, thick strands of melted cheese. I watched as she elongated the bouncy cheese curds with her hands over and over, draining the excess fluid and fat before dipping it in black nigella seeds, twisting it up into a tight figure-eight shape, and throwing it into a large vat of cold salted water. It was oddly satisfying to watch her pull the taffy-like cheese into a final perfect knot. Of course my curiosity got the best of me, and I asked her if she would teach me to make it. She respectfully declined with a smile, explaining that it was a family secret. Fair enough, but I would not be deterred.

Soon after, when I opened Tanoreen, I asked one of my prep chefs, who was from Syria, if she knew how to make string cheese. I was thrilled to discover that she did, and we promptly began making fresh batches for our customers and family. **MAKES 6–8 CHEESES**

2.4kg mozzarella or 'stretched' curd cheese (found at speciality cheese shops), sliced 1.25cm thick
1 cup nigella seeds (optional)

Heat a sauté pan over a medium heat and add a generous handful of the sliced cheese curd. Cook, stirring constantly, until the oil seeps from the curds and starts to pool in the pan, using the back of a spoon or spatula to press down on the curds. Once the curds are melted, use a slotted spoon to push the cheese into a single ball and lift it out of the pan.

Working quickly, so that the cheese doesn't cool (or else it won't stretch), use your thumbs to form a hole in the middle of the ball. With your hands, begin stretching the curd into a big loop. When you can't stretch it any further, double the loop in on itself.

Continue stretching so you have two side-by-side layers of loops. Repeat this action over and over, until you've formed a 15cm wide oval of loops. Twist the two edges of the curd in opposite directions (like wringing out a washcloth) and insert one end into the loop of the other end to form a knot.

Roll your string cheese in the nigella seeds, if using, patting them into the cheese so they stick. Place the string cheese knot into a large bowl or pan filled with cool salted water. Repeat the above steps with the remaining curds. Allow your cheeses to soak for 3–6 hours. Place on a wire rack to drain. Once the excess moisture drips away, it's ready to serve, or you can wrap it tightly in clingfilm and store it in the refrigerator for up to 4 days.

NOTE: Yes, this cheese can also be sliced, but to get the full experience, you should undo the knot and slowly shred the cheese between two fingers into very thin strands and serve the strands in a large feathery mound with cucumbers, tomatoes, and plenty of bread.

TOP: Stretching into multiple loops; twisting the loops into one rope. **BOTTOM:** Tying the rope into one knot; patting the seeds onto the cheese.

A WORLD OF ARABIC CHEESES

Cheese has been a central part of the Middle Eastern diet, not least because it was an easy commodity to come by, as most families raised their own sheep, cows or goats. That's why you'll find cheese incorporated into meals throughout the day, from breakfast (as part of a quick morning spread of bread, jam, eggs, and za'atar) to dessert (as a typical ingredient in pastries).

This book is highly representative of that ingrained love of cheese, as evidenced by my regular calls for labneh, halloumi, or kashkaval. But keep your eyes peeled if you happen upon a Middle Eastern market so you can experiment with some of the other common cheeses below.

LABNEH: Made from strained and pressed yogurt (like Greek yogurt but thicker), labneh is creamy, tangy, and spreadable, making it a great alternative to cream cheese.

KASHKAVAL: Readily found in Middle Eastern groceries, this very mild, yellow, spongy-textured cheese is commonly made from cow's or sheep's milk (or both) and is a great melter, which is why you can use it almost interchangeably with Cheddar or mozzarella.

HALLOUMI: Possibly my favourite cheese, firm and briny halloumi (made from goat's and sheep's milk) can be set directly onto a grill, where it gets browned and melty outside while retaining its shape within. It's also spectacular simply cut into cubes for my Watermelon Salad (page 73) or grated directly on top of Green Tomato Shakshuka (page 20). You can also find aged halloumi, which has been stored in brine for a long time. Just be aware that it's drier, stronger, and much saltier and should be soaked in water to reduce the salinity before use.

STRING CHEESE: Made with cow's milk and studded with nigella seeds, this Syrian speciality can be found twisted into braids or coiled into balls. As I've mentioned on page 49, the traditional way to eat it is shredded into strings and served alongside fresh vegetables and toasted bread, but a friend admits that she's cut it into cubes and served it Poutine-style as a topping for chips and gravy.

NABULSI: Highly popular in Palestine, this brined, supple sheep's milk cheese flavoured with nigella seeds and mastic is almost like a cross between Syrian string cheese and durable halloumi, as it holds together when fried in oil. It's also commonly used in knafeh, a baked, cheese-stuffed filo pastry drenched in orange blossom and rose water syrup.

JIBNEH ARABIEH: Though Greek in origin, feta has found its way into Middle Eastern cuisine. This tender white cheese – native to the Persian Gulf area – serves as an authentic (and less salty) substitute.

ACKAWI: Hailing from the Acre region of Palestine, this smooth, chewy cheese is unripened and brined, lending it a slightly salty flavour and tender texture that makes it a preferred table cheese for pairing with olives, sliced vegetables or fruit.

SHANKLISH: Basically the blue cheese of the Levant, cow's or sheep's milk shanklish has a crumbly texture and is rolled into balls before being aged and dried (the longer it sits, the more pungent it becomes). For an extra dose of flavour, the layer of natural mould that develops is removed so the cheese can be coated in herbs and spices such as Aleppo chilli or za'atar.

OIL-CURED CHILLIES
WITH WALNUT STUFFING

MAKDOUS

I'd often wondered why the dish makdous – a kind of oil-cured pickle – was made exclusively with aubergine. My mum eventually explained that aubergine works so well because its texture is like a sponge; it takes on the taste of everything you add to it, but doesn't become overwhelmed.

Well, I had some stuffing left over from a batch of aubergine makdous one day. I also had jalapeños growing in my garden, and I decided to throw some in. I tucked those chillies into the bottom of the jar and forgot all about them – until my family finished off the aubergine. What a discovery! Everyone went crazy over them. I decided to try them using poblanos as well because their skin absorbs so much flavour while managing to stay crisp. As happens so often in my kitchen, this casual experiment became a top-selling item; one that my customers will never let me take off the menu. **MAKES 1 LITRE**

9 poblano chillies, 8 whole and 1 very finely chopped

6 jalapeño chillies

Sea salt

210g chopped walnuts

6 cloves garlic, diced

1 tablespoon lemon salt (available online)

2–4 tablespoons Harissa (see page 212), to taste

4 tablespoons olive oil, plus more for filling the jar

Prepare the whole poblano and jalapeño chillies by making a narrow, lengthways slit from the stem to the tip, being careful not to cut all the way through. Remove the seeds and sprinkle with salt inside and out. Place in a covered container and leave in the refrigerator overnight. Before using, gently rinse the excess salt away with water and pat dry.

In a medium bowl, combine the walnuts, garlic, diced poblano chilli, 1 tablespoon sea salt, the lemon salt, harissa and oil. Fill the chillies with the stuffing, making sure to pack it tightly into the cavities.

Layer the chillies stem-side down in a clean 1-litre jar, alternating the jalapeños and poblanos. Press down on the chillies so they are packed tightly. While continuing to press, pour oil into the jar until it reaches just below the rim. Place clingfilm on top of the oil to seal it in, screw the top on the jar, and leave in the refrigerator to pickle for at least 3 days (although they taste even better after 5 or 6 days).

These last for a month in the refrigerator. Once you've finished with the peppers, you can use the remaining oil to start your next batch!

TOP: detaching the top of a pepper; cutting out the seeds and membranes. BOTTOM: stuffing the pepper; replacing the top.

MY PICK OF PEPPERS

Though Middle Eastern food is certainly associated with spices, it's not generally known as being hot, except for our penchant for hot pepper paste and harissa. But as you work your way through this book, you'll find that time and again, I call for sturdy, smoky poblanos (the influence of New York's vibrant Mexican population) as well as crunchy, tingly jalapeños (keep in mind that the red ones pack more of a punch than the green ones). Even more frequently I make use of long hots — also known as frying peppers — a direct effect of living in a traditionally Italian neighborhood. Yellowish, semisweet, and spindly, they're actually not terribly fiery, making it easy to adjust the heat of a dish to your taste.

As for Middle Eastern varieties, I've found them a bit harder to come by. But by all means, if you spot fresh Aleppo peppers (more commonly found dried and powdered in the spice aisle), grab them! A staple of their namesake Syrian city, Aleppo peppers have become increasingly rare due to the ravages of war. Like the country's cuisine, these brick-red beauties are packed with flavor; they are tantalizingly tart, intensely fruity and seductively aromatic all at once. Though also more readily available dried, Turkish urfa biber peppers are worth seeking out as well. Their concentrated raisin and chocolate notes add intriguing elements to savory dishes.

As with all chillies, most of the fire resides in the seeds and ribs, so by all means, remove them if you want to tone down the heat. I prefer a bit of kick in my food but I treat chillies as wholly optional in my recipes. You can omit them completely, stick with peppers, or, on the other end of the spectrum, you can go for broke with habaneros, Scotch bonnets, or ghost chillies. It's entirely up to you.

FILLET STEAK
SHAWARMA SLIDERS

When my children were younger, we spent summers in the Galilee visiting our family. On the drive from the airport to my parents' home in Nazareth, we would always stop at my favourite shawarma stand in Haifa. My mother would have a feast waiting for us at home, but I couldn't help it. A tightly wrapped sandwich with marinated lamb, pickles, harissa and tahini after a long flight was heavenly.

I'd never served shawarma at my restaurant because taking care of an enormous rotisserie spit is truly a business unto itself. And then it came to me – I would make beefed-up, appetiser-size sliders instead. They'd be simple to make, easy to eat and wouldn't ruin your appetite for a big meal. My version flips the script by swapping fillet steak for the lamb to elevate this common street food. Although it's a pricey cut of meat, a little goes a long way here. **MAKES 8 MINI PITTAS**

900g fillet steak (can substitute topside or sirloin), chopped small

1 teaspoon curry powder

1 teaspoon freshly ground black pepper

1 teaspoon ground coriander

1 teaspoon ground cumin

1 teaspoon ground turmeric

½ teaspoon ground cardamom

⅓ teaspoon freshly grated nutmeg

3 cloves garlic, diced

6 tablespoons olive oil

6 tablespoons white vinegar

Sea salt

Mini pittas, chopped red onion, chopped parsley, diced tomatoes and pickles for serving

Tahini Yogurt, Tahini Pomegranate Hot Sauce or 40 Cloves of Garlic Sauce for serving (pages 209–211)

In a large bowl, mix the fillet steak, curry powder, black pepper, coriander, turmeric, cardamom, nutmeg, garlic, oil and vinegar together to evenly coat the meat with the seasonings.

Heat a large frying pan over a medium heat, add the seasoned meat, and cook for 4–6 minutes, stirring occasionally, until cooked through to your liking. Season with salt.

Fill the pitta pockets with the meat mixture and finish with your choice of toppings and condiments.

NOTE: Pitta pockets can be swapped for wraps or lettuce cups.

GREEN ZA'ATAR PUFFS

These savoury puffs were inspired by my favourite late evening snack when I was growing up in Nazareth. We would eat our largest meal of the day in the early evening, right after my parents came home from work. This left a few hours before bed, and when we got hungry, we prepared a wrap with thin taboon bread, za'atar and crumbled halloumi cheese. It was heavenly. These puffs are a reconstructed version that uses all the same ingredients, but in one perfectly formed bite. You can serve them at a cocktail party or as part of a hearty brunch. **MAKES MAKES 36**

DOUGH

1 teaspoon active dried yeast

1 teaspoon sugar

520g plain flour, plus more as needed

110g natural yogurt, homemade (page 94) or shop-bought

1 teaspoon sea salt

½ teaspoon mastic (optional)

1 teaspoon mahlab (optional)

Olive oil, for greasing

STUFFING

225g (1 block) halloumi cheese, very finely chopped

65g chopped fresh green za'atar leaves (wild thyme, see oppostie)

2 shallots, finely chopped

2 tablespoons sumac, or the juice of 1 lemon

1 teaspoon freshly ground black pepper

1 teaspoon chilli flakes

120ml olive oil

1 long hot chilli, diced, or 1 tablespoon Harissa (page 212; optional)

Make the dough: In a small bowl, combine 120ml warm water with the sugar and yeast and set aside for 5 minutes, or until the mixture is foamy.

Combine the flour, the yeast mixture, the yogurt, salt, and mastic and mahlab, if using, in the bowl of a stand mixer fixed with a dough hook (or a large mixing bowl). Add 240ml water. Mix on low speed until the ingredients are just combined, then increase the speed to medium and mix for about 5 minutes, until the dough pulls away from the sides of the bowl, adding flour as needed if it is too wet or water if it is too dry.

Oil a large bowl and add the dough. Cover, put in a warm place, and leave for about 1 hour, until the dough is doubled in size.

Lightly oil your hands and divide the dough into 36 equal-size balls about 5cm in diameter. Let them rest on a flat surface until slightly expanded, 5–10 minutes.

While the dough is resting, preheat the oven to 200°C/gas mark 6. Lightly grease two baking trays.

Make the stuffing: Mix all the stuffing ingredients together in a large bowl.

To make the puffs, using your thumb, poke an indentation in the centre of each ball that's large enough to hold 1 tablespoon of stuffing and fill the puffs. Close the dough around the stuffing and roll it back into a ball. Let rest until slightly expanded again, 5–10 minutes, and bake until golden brown, 12–15 minutes. Serve immediately, or store at room temperature for up to 4 hours.

Green Za'atar

In describing za'atar, typically composed of ground and dried thyme, marjoram, oregano, toasted sesame seeds, salt, and perhaps some sumac, the whole is infinitely greater than the sum of its parts. Especially when sprinkled on crispy flatbread, scattered atop eggs, or used as a rub for grilled fish or roasted meats.

But if you haven't yet tried wild-growing, fresh green za'atar, you're really missing out. Not only does it go back long enough to have been found in Egyptian tombs and referenced in the Old Testament, it's considered by many to be a symbol of Palestine itself, frequently kept in homes as a hallmark of identity, heritage and culture. The shrub-like plants cover hills and farms throughout the Levant and are starting to show up in Middle Eastern markets around the world as well. Which is a fabulous thing, as fresh za'atar has all the potency of the dried spice, with a remarkably lush, grassy quality thrown into the mix as well, making it a perfect addition to salads or substitute for parsley or coriander.

Mix It Up

For easy party prep, the puffs can be baked in advance and stored in the freezer. Simply let the puffs come to room temperature for about 30 minutes before you're ready to serve, then pop into a 200°C/gas mark 6 oven for 5 minutes to reheat. On the other hand, there's no rule that you have to spend ages making individual-size puffs. When my kids were growing up, I would roll the dough into four 45cm rectangles, sprinkle the stuffing over them, leaving a 2.5cm rim around the sides, and then roll them up into logs. Want to give it a try? Simply place the logs seam-side down on a greased pan, brush with egg white, bake until golden, let rest for a bit, then cut them into thick slices.

KIBBEH CUPS

Kibbeh is the national dish of several Middle Eastern countries, and for good reason. It can be baked, fried, grilled, served raw, or smothered in a sauce or stock and it appears in multiple shapes and sizes. While traditionally made from lamb or beef, fish and chicken work just as well, and kibbeh can even go completely vegan (you'll find recipes for all of the above later in the book). This dish plays up kibbeh's versatility still further by forming it into appetiser-size cups. **MAKES ABOUT 24 KIBBEH CUPS**

FOR LAMB KIBBEH
(can also use Pumpkin, Chicken or Fish Kibbeh dough on pages 122, 136 or 166)

½ teaspoon ground allspice

⅛ teaspoon ground cumin

⅛ teaspoon freshly ground black pepper

⅛ teaspoon dried marjoram

⅛ teaspoon freshly grated nutmeg

85g coarse bulgar wheat, soaked in cold water to cover for 30 minutes

1 teaspoon sea salt

1 tablespoon Hot Pepper Paste (page 212; optional)

¼ yellow onion or 1 shallot, grated or finely chopped in a food processor

225g lean minced lamb

Vegetable oil, for frying

Fillings of your choice, such as Lemony Aubergine Hash (page 87) or Grilled Corn Salad (page 82)

Fill a bowl with ice water. In a large bowl, combine the allspice, cumin, black pepper, marjoram and nutmeg and stir in half of the soaked bulgar. Dip your hands in the ice water and let the water drip into the bulgar mixture. Using both hands, press handfuls of the mixture between your palms to incorporate the spices, pressing and pushing it away between your hands as if kneading bread. Continue dipping your hands in the ice water and allowing the water to drip in the bowl until when you squeeze a handful of the bulgar mixture in your hand it stays together.

Add the remaining bulgar, the salt, hot pepper paste, if using, the onion and the minced lamb and knead to incorporate in the same way as you first added the bulgar, until it forms a dough. Using the water to keep your hands moist, roll the dough into palm-size balls. Push an opening into the centre of each ball with your thumbs, gently widening the cavity and pushing up the edges, to form shallow cups 5–7.5cm in diameter. Set them on a baking tray and place in the freezer until solid, at least 1 hour. When you are ready to serve, pour enough oil into a pan or deep-fat fryer so that it will submerge the cups. Heat the oil until hot but not smoking. Add the kibbeh cups in batches and fry until golden, 5–7 minutes. Top with desired fillings while still warm.

NOTE: If your dough isn't sturdy enough to hold its shape, add some breadcrumbs or flour. If it's too firm, add a bit of water instead.

HALLOUMI BITES
WITH HOT TOMATO JAM

Cheese and tomato is one of my favourite food combinations. This dish is an elevated take on the grilled cheese and tomato sandwiches I ate when I was growing up. Spear the squares with toothpicks and serve these bites as hors d'oeuvres at a cocktail party. Think of them as the Syrian love child of Italian mozzarella sticks and cheese curds! **MAKES ABOUT 36 BITES**

TOMATO JAM

3 tablespoons olive oil

8 cloves garlic, finely diced

1–2 poblano or jalapeño chillies, finely diced (deseeded if you like)

½ teaspoon ground cumin

500g diced tomatoes

3 tablespoons Hot Pepper Paste (page 212)

1 tablespoon tomato purée

Juice of 1 lemon

CHEESE

1 large egg white

450g (2 blocks) halloumi cheese

115g seasoned breadcrumbs (we use ¼ teaspoon each garlic powder, dried basil, and lemon pepper)

Plain flour, for dusting

Vegetable oil, for frying

Make the jam: In a medium saucepan, heat the olive oil over a medium heat. Add the garlic, chillies and cumin and cook, stirring constantly, until softened, about 3 minutes. Add the tomatoes, cover, and cook until the tomatoes are very soft, about 15 minutes. Add the hot pepper paste, tomato purée and lemon juice and simmer, uncovered, until the sauce thickens and reduces a bit, about 10 more minutes.

Make the cheese: In a shallow bowl, beat the egg white until frothy. Cut each halloumi block in half horizontally and cut them into 5cm squares. In a second shallow bowl, combine the breadcrumbs and spices. Lightly dust the cheese cubes with flour, then toss them in the egg white, followed by the breadcrumb mixture. Pour enough vegetable oil in a frying pan to reach a depth of 1.25cm, or fill a deep-fat fryer with oil to a depth that will submerge the cheese cubes. Heat the oil until very hot, but not smoking. Fry until golden on all sides, about 4 minutes.

Serve the bites immediately with the jam on the side for dipping (reheat it if needed). The bites can also be held at room temperature for up to an hour.

NOTE: This recipe can easily be gluten-free. Just omit the breadcrumbs and fry the cheese on its own. The halloumi will fry to golden brown while holding its shape and density.

SALADS & SIDES

THE POWER OF PRODUCE

We tend to have a different definition of 'salad' in the Middle East. Instead of a big bowl piled high with leafy greens, salad is more likely an olive oil and lemon dressed melange of grains and chopped vegetables – think *tabouleh* and *fattoush*, both of which I put my spin on here.

What could be healthier than what comes from the earth? Not only are vegetables full of colour, they're packed with tons of nutritional benefits and wholly delicious in their unadorned state. Of all ingredients, produce is my favourite. In fact, I largely follow a vegetable-centric diet, with small amounts of protein scattered here and there. I could live on salads and sides, as dining on multiple smaller dishes rather than a large portion of one single thing is what suits me best.

The mission of this chapter is to relay my veggie enthusiasm to you in recipes that excite the palate. For example, Coriander Green Beans with Toasted Almonds (page 97) is far from your average bland side dish stuck in the corner of the table as a placeholder. Flash-fried and crunchy, wonderfully nutty and floral from a dose of scattered coriander seeds, it has the the potential to upstage main course dinner companions like turkey.

Why shouldn't delicacies like these move from the side to the centre? I've had so much fun expanding my repertoire past the traditional dishes I loved while growing up, to include a whole new range of vegetable- and grain-focused creations that take advantage of the wealth of ingredients now readily available.

For instance, fennel was just becoming commonplace when I was growing up in the Middle East, and I remember my mum mixing it into lentil pilafs and soups and my dad tossing fronds into a sauté. So when I first spotted fennel in the United States, those fond memories came back to me and inspired me to find interesting new ways to use it (though I still think the liquorice-flavoured bulb is at its very best raw, as in my Fennel, Pomegranate & Sage Salad, page 68).

Diamonds in the Rough

I first encountered kohlrabi and jicama after living in New York. They both look a bit intimidating — especially knobby kohlrabi — but I came to adore their crunchy and juicy qualities. So I peeled, shredded and pickled them (because I pickle almost every vegetable I can think of), and found they also make an especially sturdy addition to salads. These two veg taught me a lesson that can be applied to almost any ingredient: if you have the guts to bring something new home and try it, a whole new culinary horizon will open to you. Here's some advice on using these earthy gems:

All parts of kohlrabi, a bulbous member of the cabbage family, are edible. Chop off the stems and leaves if still attached (reserve them for a stir-fry or soup) as well as the tough root end. Use a small, sharp paring knife to cut away any protruding, knobby bits and peel the thick skin with a vegetable peeler.

Jicama isn't available in the UK, so you could substitute for 1 large daikon radsh, peeled and cut into thin matchsticks to use.

CORIANDER SALATA

I personally adore coriander, but am aware of how polarising an ingredient it can be. No matter where you fall on the coriander spectrum, however, I urge you to try this vibrant salad, which just may change your mind about the fragrant herb.

This truly tastes like summer in a bowl, yet is made with ingredients that are available year-round. The salad makes a wonderful stand-in for chimichurri on top of fish, grilled meat or chicken, but it is delicious when enjoyed all on its own! **MAKES 2–4 SERVINGS**

80g chopped coriander leaves

2 poblano chillies, deseeded, cut into quarters, and thinly sliced

1 lime, peel and pith removed with a knife, cut into quarters, and thinly sliced

1 red onion, cut into quarters and thinly sliced

Juice of 2 lemons

75ml olive oil

1 teaspoon sea salt

½ teaspoon freshly ground black pepper

10 stoned kalamata olives

1 avocado, peeled and thinly sliced

In a large bowl, combine the coriander, chillies, lime and onion. In a small bowl, whisk the lemon juice, oil, salt and pepper. Pour the dressing over the coriander and toss gently, so as not to bruise the delicate leaves. Garnish with the olives and avocado slices and serve.

FENNEL, POMEGRANATE & SAGE SALAD

Thick-cut wedges of fresh fennel (shomar in Arabic) topped with its own feathery fronds, a squeeze of lemon, and a generous pinch of good salt is one of my all-time favourite nibbles in the summer. This recipe transforms that snack into a salad by balancing the aromatic anise flavour of fennel with briny olives and sweet pomegranate seeds and adding a punchy dressing that does little to diminish the vegetable's celery-like crunch. This is summery, barbecue-friendly food at its best. **MAKES 4–6 SERVINGS**

SALAD

4 fennel bulbs, cored and cut into thin strips, fronds reserved

1 poblano chilli, diced

50g kalamata olives, stoned

10g fresh coriander leaves

1 clove garlic, crushed

1 tablespoon chopped fresh dill

12g finely chopped fresh sage (or 1 tablespoon dried sage)

150g fresh pomegranate seeds (optional)

DRESSING

2 tablespoons balsamic vinegar

5 tablespoons fresh lemon juice (about 1 large lemon)

5 tablespoons olive oil

½ teaspoon freshly ground black pepper

Sea salt

125g crumbled feta cheese (optional)

Make the salad: In a large bowl, toss together the fennel, chilli, olives, coriander, garlic, dill, sage and pomegranate seeds.

Make the dressing: In a small bowl, whisk the vinegar, lemon juice and oil until emulsified. Add the pepper and season with salt. Toss the dressing with the vegetables.

To serve, arrange the reserved fennel fronds around the edges of a platter. Place the salad in the centre and top with the cheese, if using. (Alternatively, you can garnish with the fennel fronds and add lemon slices or a drizzle of balsamic vinegar).

BITTER GREENS
WITH SWEET TAHINI DRESSING

This dish showcases the incredible diversity of my beloved Tahini Pomegranate Sauce. The dressing calms the assertive flavour and tames the brawny texture of unusual, nutrient-packed greens like dandelion (most commonly used in the Middle East for sautés and stews), watercress (which has a gently peppery profile), and chicory (which adds a slight bite like tenderstem broccoli). It's definitely more than a mere dressing here — at once tangy, sweet, and rich, yet light and fruity, adding intriguing elements to an otherwise predominantly bitter salad.

This dish can be pulled together in minutes for lunch, dinner, or even a big party if you do what I do — make bulk amounts of dressing in advance. Like most of my sauces, Tahini Pomegranate keeps beautifully in the refrigerator for two to three weeks, and in the freezer almost indefinitely. **MAKES 6-8 SERVINGS**

1 bunch endive, roughly chopped

1 bunch dandelion greens, roughly chopped

1 bunch watercress, roughly chopped

Sea salt

2 plum tomatoes or 1 large tomato, chopped

240ml Tahini Pomegranate Hot Sauce (page 209),
    or to taste

Cucumber slices, red onion slices, and/or
    1 chopped long hot chilli, for serving

Place the greens in a colander and toss with a sprinkle of salt. Let sit for 10 minutes, rinse the salt off with water, and gently squeeze with your hands to release excess water and remove some of the bitterness.

In a salad bowl, toss the greens with the tomatoes and Tahini Pomegranate Hot Sauce. Top with cucumber, red onion, and/or chilli and serve.

LEAVE THE LETTUCE

If salads are considered the ultimate in healthy eating, why are so many of them based on iceberg and cos? Don't get me wrong, lettuce definitely has its place. But not only does it tend to wilt under the weight of dressing and other ingredients, it doesn't actually bring that much to the bowl in terms of health benefits. So consider giving the following nourishing greens a go in your next toss.

BEETROOT GREENS: My love of beetroot is well known, but I'd never dream of tossing out the tender, sweet-tasting greens — especially since they harbour impressive amounts of protein and vitamins.

ENDIVE: The root (called chicory in the US) is a popular addition — or substitute — to coffee in Louisiana (it has a creamy mouth-feel like milk, yet actually reduces stress and settles the stomach, unlike caffeine), and the leaves are worth attention as well. Tangy and a little bit woody, the ruffled, vitamin-rich scoops more than stand up to heavy dressings. The same goes for endive's toothsome cousins, Belgian endive and radicchio.

DANDELION: So much more than an invasive weed, dandelion greens are chock-full of calcium and iron and help control inflammation. They're a go-to side dish in our kitchen (simply sautéed in garlic and oil) but equally intriguing in salads, thanks to their pronounced, peppery bite.

MUSTARD GREENS: Totally over kale? Consider giving mustard a try. Just gently massage the tough leaves with salt or olive oil first, before incorporating them into a salad; they'll bring lots of fibre and magnesium.

KALE: This curly cabbage may be in danger of becoming over exposed, but what could be hipper than being healthy? Not only is kale a nutrient superstar (essentially checking down the alphabet when it comes to vitamins), it's especially high in lutein, an antioxidant that aids eyesight.

SPINACH: It seems Popeye was well ahead of this diet trend. Just don't get your greens from a tin, as cooking supple spinach (which is native to Persia, by the way) can leach away its stores of beta-carotene, alpha-lipoic acid and iron.

SWISS CHARD: This rainbow-stalked, wholly edible green counts amaranth and quinoa as relatives. Talk about a fit family!

WATERCRESS: Grown atop beds of water, cress may seem mild and delicate, but don't be fooled; it produces nutrients that may help protect against cancer.

WATERMELON, HALLOUMI & ZA'ATAR SALAD

During hot Nazareth summers, my mother would forgo making laborious meals over the hob and prepare a cooling spread of mezze for a light supper instead. She would lay out ripe wedges of watermelon, firm halloumi, crispy cucumber, briny olives, warm hunks of bread and grapes from our own vines.

This recipe is so much more than the now ubiquitous watermelon-feta salad. It's my mother's famous summertime mezze all tossed together in one bowl.

And, of course, as with many mezze, you can switch it up any way you wish by adding other seasonal ingredients such as fresh figs, dialling the heat factor up or down, or swapping the halloumi for goat's cheese. **MAKES 4–6 SERVINGS**

225g (1 block) halloumi cheese,
    cut into 1.25cm cubes

50g stoned black olives

20g fresh green za'atar leaves (wild thyme, see page
    59), not chopped

2 shallots, diced

1 tablespoon sumac

Juice of 1 lemon

Juice of 1 lime

6 tablespoons olive oil

½ teaspoon finely diced fresh chilli such as
    jalapeño (optional)

Sea salt

1.35kg watermelon, deseeded and cut into
    2.5cm cubes

150g seedless black grapes

1 large or 2 small cucumbers, peeled and
    roughly chopped

In a large bowl, combine the cheese, olives, za'atar leaves, shallots, sumac, lemon juice, lime juice, oil and chilli, if using. Season with salt. Arrange the watermelon, grapes and cucumber in a large serving bowl, add the cheese mixture, and serve.

FREEKEH SALAD
WITH SPRING VEGETABLES

So many ingredients currently celebrated as superfoods have their origins in the Middle East. And while lentils are familiar to most of us, it's a pleasure seeing freekeh — or smoked wheat — recently receive the widespread recognition it deserves. This salad illustrates precisely what inspired me to write a second book. I got excited about taking some of our best-known, naturally healthy foods and presenting them in lively new ways.

Freekeh is traditionally prepared as a pilaf of sorts with chicken or meat, and lentils often become mujadara with caramelised onions (or fennel, as my mum preferred) and rice. But these robust, nutty ingredients are just as eager to soak up spring and summer flavours. Their earthiness and smokiness provide gorgeous contrast to handfuls of aromatic herbs, the cool anise bite of fresh fennel, and, of course, liberal amounts of lemon and olive oil. On its own it's a vegan salad, or you can make a meal out of it by serving it under a piece of grilled fish. **MAKES 6–8 SERVINGS**

SALAD

225g freekeh, rinsed

1 fennel bulb, cored and diced

3 tablespoons chopped fresh dill

3 tablespoons chopped fresh flat-leaf parsley

10g chopped fresh coriander

60g deseeded, diced long hot or jalapeño chillies

1 small red onion, diced

50g stoned finely diced black or green olives

1 tablespoon ground cumin

DRESSING

6 tablespoons olive oil

Juice of 1–2 lemons

2 cloves garlic, finely chopped

1 teaspoon sea salt, or to taste

20–25 cherry tomatoes, halved, for serving

Make the salad: Place the freekeh in a medium saucepan and add water to cover by a few inches. Bring to the boil and cook for 15–20 minutes, until tender. Drain and set aside to cool.

In a large bowl, mix the freekeh with the fennel, dill, parsley, coriander, chilli, onion, olives and cumin.

Make the dressing: In a small bowl, whisk the dressing ingredients until emulsified. Add the dressing to the salad and toss to coat. Taste and add more salt or lemon juice if needed. Garnish with the cherry tomatoes and serve.

NOTE: Because freekeh is sturdy, this salad can last a few days in the refrigerator. In fact, it often tastes better the second day, once the flavours have had a chance to marry. Feel free to swap the freekeh for small brown lentils for a grain-free variation.

CRUNCHY KOHLRABI & JICAMA SLAW

I frequently find inspiration outside of my personal culinary comfort zone. Which is how I came to appreciate kohlrabi and jicama, after spotting them at produce stands at international markets.

Since they're both texturally sturdy but a bit of a blank canvas, they really allow you to go to town flavourwise. Which is precisely what I did here, by tossing matchsticks with fresh herbs, piquant pesto, jalapeno (you know how I love things spicy!) and even a smattering of gorgeous, seasonal green almonds – a delicacy in the Middle East.

The best part is, this slaw just gets better the longer it sits. The kohlrabi and jicama soften up just a tad, and the flavours really meld together. **MAKES 4–6 SERVINGS**

SLAW

2 kohlrabis, peeled and cut into thin julienne

1 large jicama or green apple, peeled and cut into thin julienne

1 large leek, white part only, cut into thin julienne

3 whole spring onions, chopped

15 green almonds or whole toasted almonds, cut in half

1 long hot or jalapeño chilli, deseeded and diced (optional)

25g chopped fresh basil

DRESSING

3 tablespoons Coriander-Basil Pesto (page 216) or shop-bought pesto

1 shallot, diced

1 clove garlic, crushed

12g chopped fresh sage

2 tablespoons chopped fresh dill

Juice of 2 lemons

75ml olive oil

1 teaspoon sea salt

Chilli flakes, or 2 tablespoons chilli oil (optional)

2–4 halved and cored peppers, for serving

Make the slaw: In a large bowl, toss together the kohlrabi, jicama or apple, leeks, spring onions, green almonds, shallots, chilli and basil.

Make the dressing: In a small bowl, whisk together the pesto, shallot, garlic, sage, dill, lemon juice, oil, salt and crushed chilli flakes, if using. Pour over the vegetable mixture and toss well to combine. Serve the slaw by mounding it into the cavities of the halved peppers.

GREEN (FRESH) ALMONDS: You'll find these fuzzy, fruity, emerald-coloured nuts right at the start of spring, harvested before they mature into the hard, brown, buttery almonds that most of us are familiar with. While they are a great component within many dishes, you can also simply pop them in your mouth whole, perhaps tossed with good olive oil and a dusting of sea salt. You can buy them online.

AUTUMN FATTOUSH

As I was writing this book, summer turned to autumn, and the leaves started to change colours. I thought about our family's yearly trip upstate to see nature's seasonal show and was inspired to create this autumn-themed salad. My son suggested I use fattoush – that sumac-sprinkled, pitta chip-filled quintessential bread salad found on just about every mezze spread – as a jumping-off point, and that's how this vibrant salad, flush with crimson cabbage, radicchio and beetroot was born. **MAKES 6–8 SERVINGS**

SALAD

120g shredded red cabbage

3 heads radicchio, coarsely chopped

1 small beetroot, peeled and shredded

6 radishes, thinly sliced

1 red onion, quartered and thinly sliced

2 medium tomatoes, diced

Handful of pomegranate seeds

140g toasted pitta chips

DRESSING

4 tablespoons fresh lemon juice

4 tablespoons olive oil

1 clove garlic, finely diced

2 tablespoons sumac

1 teaspoon dried mint

Sea salt to taste

Combine the salad ingredients in a large bowl. In a small bowl, whisk the dressing ingredients until thoroughly emulsified (or shake them in a covered jar). Pour the dressing over the salad, toss well to coat and serve.

The Pitta Chip Tip

Making your own toasted pitta chips is simple: Tear pitta bread into pieces, drizzle with olive oil, and crisp in a 230°C/gas mark 8 oven.

QUINOA TABOULEH

While quinoa teeters on the edge of overexposure, I always appreciate using ancient ingredients in modern ways. There's no question that quinoa's moment in the sun is well deserved. It's protein-packed, fibre-rich, and gluten-free, a truly nutritionally blessed wonder food.

While the Middle East is flush with good-for-you grains (such as that smoky powerhouse, freekeh), I only came into contact with quinoa a few years ago. My son, now a Californian, visited us one summer. For dinner one night, he prepared quinoa salad, which had a wonderful, almost caviar-like texture that absorbed the dressing beautifully without getting soggy or dry. When he began to tell me about its health benefits, I was completely sold.

I immediately got into the kitchen and cooked up a plain batch of quinoa just to get a sense of how it tasted unadorned. I was underwhelmed, and found it a bit bland. What that quinoa needed was to be dressed up. Black-tie dressed up. When I considered quinoa as a flavour-delivery vessel with tremendous health benefits, my imagination took over. I used it in tabouleh instead of cracked wheat to make the time-honoured salad gluten-free. This dish started my love affair with quinoa and inspired me to incorporate it again and again in my recipes. **MAKES 8–10 SERVINGS**

QUINOA
180ml olive oil
2 shallots, diced
3 cloves garlic, diced
½ teaspoon sea salt
Pinch of freshly ground black pepper
1 teaspoon ground cumin
250g quinoa
360ml boiling water or vegetable or chicken stock

SALAD
80g chopped fresh flat-leaf parsley
25g chopped fresh coriander
15g chopped fresh mint
2 Kirby or Persian cucumbers, diced
3 plum tomatoes, diced
1 large fennel bulb, cored and diced (reserve 2 fronds for serving)
1 long hot chilli, deseeded and chopped (optional)
1 small red onion, diced

3 spring onions, green parts only, chopped
120ml olive oil
Juice of 2 large lemons (about 120ml)
1 teaspoon sea salt, or to taste
Pinch of freshly ground black pepper

Make the quinoa: In a deep frying pan, heat the oil over a medium heat. Add the shallots and cook for 2–3 minutes, until the shallots are golden. Add the garlic and cook until aromatic, then add the salt, black pepper and cumin. Add the quinoa and boiling water and bring to the boil. Reduce the heat and simmer for 12 minutes, or until the quinoa is cooked through. Remove from the heat and spread over a baking tray to cool.

Assemble the salad: Place the quinoa in a large bowl and add the parsley, coriander, mint, cucumbers, tomatoes, fennel, chilli, if using, onion and spring onions and toss to combine. Add the oil, lemon juice, salt and pepper and serve garnished with the fennel fronds.

GRILLED SWEETCORN SALAD

My son, Tarek, challenged me to try to make succotash, a dish I had never heard of before. After some experimentation, I chose fresh summer sweetcorn as the base and passed on the lima beans in favour of lots of fresh herbs and grilled seasonal vegetables, plus Middle Eastern seasonings such as coriander. The dish is equally wonderful next to grilled meat, with leftovers packed in your lunchbox for the next day.

MAKES 6–8 SERVINGS

8 ears of fresh sweetcorn

4 Arabic squash, summer squash, or courgettes, thickly sliced

2 kohlrabis, peeled and sliced into rounds

2 large waxy potatoes, peeled and sliced into rounds

1 poblano chilli, sliced lengthways

2 beefsteak tomatoes, thickly sliced into rounds

3 shallots, sliced lengthways

2 tablespoons olive oil, plus more for brushing

3 cloves garlic, diced

20g chopped fresh coriander

25g chopped fresh basil

1 tablespoon ground coriander

1 tablespoon freshly ground black pepper

Juice of 2 lemons

1½ tablespoons sea salt, or to taste

Brush all the vegetables with oil and grill them on a barbecue or griddle pan until tender and lightly charred. Cut the corn off the cob and cut the remaining vegetables into uniform, corn kernel–size dice and set aside.

In a large sauté pan, heat the oil over a medium heat. Add the garlic and cook until fragrant, about 2 minutes. Add the coriander, basil, coriander and black pepper and stir to combine. Add the lemon juice, salt and the grilled vegetables and heat over a low heat until warmed through. Serve the salad warm or cold.

No Grill?
No Problem
If you don't have a barbecue or griddle pan (or just don't feel like dealing with the smoke), the olive oil-rubbed vegetables can be roasted in a 230ºC/gas mark 8 oven until caramelised and tender, about 30 minutes.

ARTICHOKE & TOMATO SAUTÉ
WITH PESTO

On his first visit to Tanoreen, one of our regular customers tried these sautéed artichoke hearts. That was over a decade and a half ago, and he still calls ahead to request it, most recently for his ninety-first birthday celebration. This simple side pairs well with many dishes, but I especially love it alongside Pan-roasted Salmon with Salsa Khadra (page 159). **MAKES 6–8 SERVINGS**

75ml olive oil

1.2kg artichoke hearts, sliced

3 cloves garlic, chopped

1 tablespoon sea salt

1 teaspoon freshly ground black pepper

1 tablespoon ground coriander

8 plum tomatoes, diced

1 tablespoon fresh lemon juice

8 tablespoons Coriander-Basil Pesto (page 216)
    or shop-bought pesto

Fresh basil leaves, for garnish

In a large saucepan, heat the oil over a medium heat. Add the sliced artichoke hearts and cook for 7–10 minutes, until golden brown. Add the garlic, salt, black pepper and coriander and cook for 2–3 minutes. Add the tomatoes, lemon juice and pesto and cook until the artichoke hearts and tomatoes are softened, about 5 minutes. Serve garnished with basil leaves.

QUINOA PILAF
WITH ROASTED VEGETABLES
SHULBATO

When I was growing up, my mother would make shulbato (bulgar cooked with tomato sauce and aubergine) with vegetables picked fresh from our gardens. Since it's wonderful eaten at room temperature or even cold, it's perfect for taking on a picnic or, back in the day, olive picking in the countryside. As I did with my tabouleh (page 81), I swapped quinoa for the traditional bulgar wheat to make the dish gluten-free. The quinoa absorbs the tomato and all those wonderful spices, making this the kind of healthy eating that's easy to stick with! **MAKES 4–6 SERVINGS**

1 large Italian aubergine, cut into 2.5cm cubes

240ml olive oil

2 large shallots, chopped

1 clove garlic, chopped

1 poblano chilli, chopped

3 Arabic squash or 1 large courgette, cut into
    2.5cm cubes

340g quinoa

5 teaspoons tomato purée

960ml tomato juice

1 teaspoon ground cumin

1 teaspoon sea salt

1 teaspoon freshly ground black pepper

Preheat the oven to 230°C/gas mark 8.

Toss the aubergine with 60ml of the oil, spread on a baking tray, and roast for 25 minutes.

Meanwhile, heat the remaining 180ml oil in a large, deep sauté pan over a medium heat. Add the shallots and garlic and cook until softened, about 6 minutes. Add the chilli and squash and cook for 5–7 minutes. Add the quinoa, aubergine, tomato purée, tomato juice, cumin, salt and pepper and stir to combine. Bring to a simmer, then cover, reduce the heat to low, and cook for about 25 minutes, until the quinoa is tender and has absorbed all the liquid. Serve warm or at room temperature.

NOTE: Shred your favourite cheese on top just after plating. Chilli Cheddar would add a great kick!

WARM ORZO
WITH ARTICHOKE HEARTS

My associations with orzo are not with Greece, but actually my mother's own Middle Eastern kitchen. When we were young, she would brown and toast dry orzo in butter for the rice pilaf commonly made with vermicelli.

Since it's so good at absorbing the flavours you pair it with, I was inspired to make this warm salad, chock-full of jammy sun-dried tomatoes, robust caramelised artichokes and lemon juice-enlivened pesto that perfectly coats each diamond-shaped grain of pasta.

A regular customer celebrating his ninetieth birthday was in the restaurant on the first night I served this dish. He was so won over by it that he now calls ahead for it. That's when you know a dish is good enough to keep on the menu! **MAKES 6–8 SERVINGS**

785g artichoke hearts, sliced

345ml olive oil

2 shallots, diced

6 cloves garlic, diced

1 tablespoon freshly ground black pepper

265g orzo pasta

5 plum tomatoes, peeled and diced

10 medium white mushrooms, thinly sliced

110g oil-packed sun-dried tomatoes, chopped

25g chopped fresh basil

120g roughly chopped baby spinach

720ml boiling water

80g shredded Parmesan cheese (optional)

3 tablespoons Coriander-Basil Pesto (page 216) or shop-bought pesto

Juice of 1 lemon

1 teaspoon sea salt

Preheat the oven to 230°C/gas ,mark 8. Toss the artichokes with 120ml of the olive oil, spread in a single layer on a baking tray, and roast until caramelised and tender, 15–20 minutes.

In the meantime, heat 150ml of the oil in a large sauté pan over a medium heat. Add the shallots and cook for 6–8 minutes. Add the garlic and cook for 2–3 minutes. Stir in the black pepper and orzo and cook for 2 minutes. Add the plum tomatoes and cook for 3–5 minutes, until the tomatoes are wilted. Add the mushrooms, sun-dried tomatoes, basil and spinach, stir to combine, and cook for another 2–3 minutes. Add the boiling water and artichoke hearts and bring to the boil. Reduce the heat to low, cover, and simmer for 15 minutes, checking halfway through and adding 60ml additional water if the mixture is dry, until the orzo is al dente. Remove from the heat. Stir in the cheese, if using, the pesto, lemon juice, salt, and the remaining 75ml oil and serve.

NOTE: As my mum discovered, orzo provides a wonderful textural contrast when mixed with rice, but it's also a good substitute for it, and vice versa. So you could easily swap in basmati rice here or try a plate of buttered orzo as a base for one of my saucy meat stews.

AUBERGINE HASH
WITH TOMATOES

There is no doubt that this salad is spectacular on its own, but tucked into warm kibbeh cups (page 60) it truly transforms, revealing a glorious contrast in texture and temperature. Oh, and the answer is yes, you can roast the aubergine instead of frying. Just toss with olive oil and roast for 25–30 minutes in a 200°C/gas mark 6 oven. **MAKES 960ML**

120ml vegetable oil

1 large Italian aubergine, cut into 2.5cm cubes

330g peeled diced tomato

3 cloves garlic, finely chopped

1 red onion, finely diced

2 spring onions, chopped

2 Persian or Kirby cucumbers, cubed

6 tablespoons olive oil

120ml fresh lemon juice

Sea salt

Put the vegetable oil in a large frying pan, and place it over a medium heat until hot but not smoking. Add the aubergine, working in batches if necessary, and fry until it is tender and brown on all sides, 5–8 minutes. Remove the aubergine with a slotted spoon and let it drain on kitchen paper.

Place the aubergine in a large bowl and add the tomato, garlic, red and spring onions and cucumber. In a small bowl, whisk the oil and lemon juice and season with salt. Pour the dressing over the salad and toss well to combine. Chill in the refrigerator before using.

EXTRA CREDIT: Slices of grilled rustic bread brushed with olive oil and topped with the aubergine hash and crumbles of feta cheese make a fantastic crostini.

NOTE: To release some of the aubergine's bitterness, place it in a colander, toss with salt, and let sit for 15 minutes, then rinse and pat dry before using it.

How to Peel a Tomato

The thought of peeling a fresh tomato may send you running for a tin. But I implore you to drop that tin opener! While removing the skins with the goal of a silky sauce or smooth salad might seem like a drag, I promise it will only take seconds of your time, and the effort will pay off dividends.

STEP 1: Bring a pan of water to the boil. Place a bowl of ice water directly next to it.

STEP 2: With a paring knife, cut a shallow X in the stem end of each tomato.

STEP 3: Using a slotted spoon, carefully lower the tomatoes into the boiling water. Once the skins begin to wrinkle and peel away from the stems, about 30 seconds, remove the tomatoes with the slotted spoon and place them directly in the ice water to cool.

STEP 4: Remove the tomatoes from the water and slip the skins off the tomatoes.

TANGY ROASTED ROOT VEGETABLES
WITH GOAT'S CHEESE

I am passionate about root vegetables, the life force of the leaves growing above. How can that not be healthy? Roots are so versatile; you can pickle them or juice them, roast them or enjoy some raw. And you can assemble any assortment you please for this salad. I especially like potatoes and turnips because they absorb the dressing like sponges. This recipe marries warm-from-the-oven roots with a crumbled coating of cool goat's cheese for a texture and temperature juxtaposition that's truly intoxicating. Since it's easy to make in big batches and a perfect autumn starter or side, this dish makes a great addition to a holiday buffet table at home, or an ideal bring-along for a potluck party. Extra dressing can be used as a sandwich spread or dip. **MAKES 6–8 SERVINGS**

ROOTS

2 medium turnips

2 medium kohlrabis

2 medium carrots

2 medium waxy potatoes

2 leeks, white parts only

180ml olive oil

1 tablespoon sea salt

1 tablespoon freshly ground black pepper

1 tablespoon ground coriander

DRESSING

2 shallots

1 poblano chilli, roughly chopped

5 cloves garlic

2 fresh sage leaves

120ml fresh lemon juice

120ml olive oil

2 tablespoons pomegranate molasses

2 tablespoons Hot Pepper Paste (page 212)

225g soft goat's cheese, to serve

Preheat the oven to 200°C/gas mark 6.

Roast the roots: Slice the turnips, kohlrabi, carrots, potatoes and leeks into 1.25cm-thick rounds and place them in a large bowl. Whisk the salt, black pepper and coriander into the oil. Place on baking trays in a single layer and brush with the spiced oil. Roast for 20–25 minutes, or until tender.

Meanwhile, make the dressing: Chop the shallots, poblano, garlic and sage in a food processor. Add the lemon juice, oil, pomegranate molasses and hot pepper paste and process until well combined. Set aside.

Place the vegetables in a serving bowl (they can be kept large or cut into smaller pieces, as you like; I julienne them). Toss with dressing to coat. Crumble the goat's cheese on top and serve warm or at room temperature.

PAN-ROASTED POTATOES & LEEKS
WITH TEKLAI

Simple roasted potatoes can be spectacular, but I strive for transcendent. For a side dish, these leeky potatoes – spuds supplemented with caramelised leeks, poblano chillies, and a garlicky, aromatic cumin-coriander pan sauce called *teklai* – are truly an attention getter. The dish is part of my regular rotation at home, as it works sensationally aside a steak or under fish. It can also replace your standard fried potatoes for brunch, or you could even tuck them into a shawarma sandwich! **MAKES 6–8 SERVINGS**

150ml olive oil

2 shallots, chopped

1 long hot or poblano chilli, sliced (optional)

6 cloves garlic, diced

6 waxy potatoes (I prefer new potatoes), peeled, cut in half, and cut into very thin julienne

6 leeks, white parts only, thinly sliced crossways

1 tablespoon freshly ground black pepper

1½ teaspoons ground cumin

2 tablespoons ground coriander

25g chopped fresh coriander

Juice of 1 lemon

Sea salt

In a large nonstick sauté pan, heat 120ml of the oil over a medium heat. Add the shallots and cook for 4 minutes, or until fragrant. Add the chilli and cook for 2 minutes, until just tender. Add 1 tablespoon of the garlic and cook until it starts to colour. Add the potatoes and leeks, reduce the heat to low, and cook for about 30 minutes, stirring frequently and gently, until the potatoes begin to soften and the leeks begin to colour.

In a small sauté pan, heat the remaining 2 tablespoons oil over a medium heat. Add the remaining 1 tablespoon garlic, the black pepper, cumin, ground coriander and fresh coriander, and cook until fragrant, about 1 minute. Pour this mixture (called *teklai*) over the potato and leeks. Turn the heat off and gently stir in the lemon juice. Season with salt and serve.

How to Roast Vegetables

If you think you don't like vegetables, chances are you've never had them roasted. While steaming or boiling can make vegetables waterlogged, weak and totally unappealing, roasting intensifies and locks in the natural flavour of the vegetable, whether it's earthy beetroot for houmous or sugary carrots, creamy kohlrabi or buttery potatoes for this salad. I always set my oven to 260°C/ gas mark 10 and cut my vegetables into uniform pieces so that they cook evenly and are tender in the middle and deeply caramelised on all sides. And while nothing more than a coating of olive oil, salt, and pepper is needed, I often add a little cumin for a toasty note.

LEBANESE SPICY PAN-FRIED POTATOES

BATATA HARRAH

This is one of my very favourite side dishes, a traditional Lebanese way of preparing potatoes tossed in heavily spiced oil (by turns fiery and flavourful). I especially love it as part of a steak dinner paired with my Fennel, Pomegranate & Sage Salad (page 68). **MAKES 4–6 SERVINGS**

120ml olive oil

8 new potatoes, peeled and cut into 2.5cm-long, 1.25cm-wide pieces

6 cloves garlic, crushed

1 red chilli, finely diced

10g fresh coriander

1 to 2 tablespoons Hot Pepper Paste (page 212 or shop-bought)

½ teaspoon ground cumin

1 teaspoon freshly ground black pepper

Juice of 4 lemons

Sea salt

In a large frying pan, heat the oil over a high heat. When it is very hot, add the potatoes and leave them until they are lightly browned on the bottom, 5–8 minutes. Turn the potatoes over, cover and cook for 3 minutes. Uncover and slightly tilt the pan so that the oil drips to the bottom of the pan and the potatoes remain at the top. Add the garlic, chilli and coriander to the oil and cook for 2 minutes, until fragrant. Stir the hot pepper paste into the potatoes. Add the cumin, black pepper and lemon juice and season with salt. Stir until the potatoes are thoroughly coated and serve.

NOTE: If you use tender red potatoes and quickly blanch them before sautéing, this dish will come together even faster.

SQUASH WITH CHICKPEAS
IN MINTED YOGURT

They say that necessity is the mother of invention. That proverb couldn't have rung more true for our family of seven. Watching my mother's thrift and creativity as she prepared fulfilling, nutritionally balanced food for a crowd every night was the only cooking school I ever needed.

I learned from my mother the value of a well-stocked pantry and how to combine few ingredients for a big flavour payoff. This mint-scented squash and chickpea dish is a reflection of both. The recipe is made with ingredients that Middle Eastern families would have already had on hand – from wholesome yogurt to plentiful, protein-packed chickpeas, supple garden squash, and fresh and dried herbs. Of course, not all of us have the luxury of shopping straight from our backyards, but you'll still find that this dish barely makes a dent in your wallet at the supermarket.

It's no secret that I love everything to do with lemon, so a scattering of zest over the top certainly wouldn't be amiss here. And the squash can be enjoyed in so many ways – as a chilled soup for supper on a hot summer evening, a cold appetiser, or a hot vegetarian stew piled over rice pilaf for a warming vegetarian meal. **MAKES 6–8 SERVINGS**

150ml olive oil

2 shallots, diced

10 baby onions, peeled

1 teaspoon freshly ground white or black pepper

1 tablespoon sea salt

1 teaspoon ground cumin

Pinch of freshly grated nutmeg

10 small Arabic squash or 5 medium courgettes, cut into 1.25cm pieces

2 tablespoons cornflour

850g low-fat natural yogurt, homemade (page 94) or shop-bought

400g tinned chickpeas, rinsed and heated with 2 tablespoons vegetable oil

3 cloves garlic, finely chopped

½ teaspoon dried mint

15g chopped fresh mint

In a large frying pan, heat 120ml of the oil over a medium heat. Add the shallots and cook until fragrant, about 3 minutes. Add the onions, pepper, salt, cumin and nutmeg and cook until onions are tender and golden, about 10 minutes. Add the squash, cover, and cook for 5 minutes, until squash is tender and golden. Turn the heat off and set aside.

In a small bowl, mix the cornflour with just enough yogurt to make a paste. Heat the remaining yogurt in a large saucepan over a medium heat until it just starts to get warm, then add the cornflour paste and stir to combine. Cook until the yogurt starts to thicken and boil at the edges, about 5 minutes. Add the chickpeas and reduce the heat to a simmer.

In a small frying pan, heat the remaining 2 tablespoons oil over a medium heat. Add the garlic and cook until lightly browned, about 2 minutes. Add the dried mint. Bring the yogurt back to the boil and stir in the mint mixture. Boil for 2 minutes, taste, and add more salt if needed. Add the squash mixture and stir once to combine. Boil for 1 minute and remove from the heat. Serve topped with the fresh mint.

HOMEMADE YOGURT

I always make my own yogurt, and though I don't expect all of you to follow my lead, you might want to give it a try. Why? Because most yogurts you'll find at the supermarket have far fewer nutritional benefits than homemade. And while I know many people sing the praises of Greek yogurt, I'm not a big fan. I find it too thick and often overpowering.

Yogurt-making opens up a world of possibilities. And don't be afraid if your first batch doesn't come out perfectly. With practice, it will become second nature. Use direct-set, single-use culture starter sachets if you're making yogurt for the first time or you are using raw milk. After that, use 100g of a previous batch of homemade yogurt. **MAKES 4½ LITRES**

4 litres milk (I like using low-fat milk or goat's milk)
1 packet culture starter (see recipe intro)

Heat the milk in a large, heavy saucepan over a medium heat, stirring constantly to make sure it doesn't scorch on the bottom. Warm the milk until it's just below boiling, it should read about 93°C on a sugar thermometer. Remove the milk from the heat and cool to 44°C–46°C, stirring occasionally to prevent a skin from forming.

Place the starter in a bowl. Pour about 250ml of the warm milk into the bowl and stir until completely incorporated. Pour the starter mixture into the pan of milk and stir again until completely incorporated. Cover the pan, turn the oven light (but not the heat) on, place the pan in the oven, and leave for at least 4 hours or overnight, until it is set to your desired consistency. Stir any watery whey that rises to the surface into the yogurt and pack the yogurt into containers. The yogurt will keep in the refrigerator for about 2 weeks.

SPICY FRYING PAN-CRUSTED RICE

In our house, we always fought over ikhatta, the crispy, intensely flavoured bits stuck to the bottom of the rice pan. So I thought, why not make a dish that's essentially nothing but ikhatta? Although you can use any deep frying pan, a wok works perfectly for creating a thick, golden sear on all sides. Drizzle the edges with a little more oil if you want the crust to be even crispier and thicker. **MAKES 4–6 SERVINGS**

165ml olive oil

2 shallots, diced

1 jalapeño chilli, deseeded and diced

3 cloves garlic, chopped

350g basmati rice

10g chopped fresh coriander

1 tablespoon ground turmeric

½ teaspoon freshly ground black pepper

1 tablespoon sea salt

3 whole cardamom pods, crushed

1 litre tomato juice, preferably fresh

2 tablespoons Hot Pepper Paste (page 212)

In a wide, deep nonstick frying pan, heat 120ml of the oil over a medium heat. Add the shallots and cook until golden brown, about 3 minutes. Add the jalapeño and garlic and cook for 2 minutes, until fragrant. Add the rice, coriander, turmeric, black pepper, salt and cardamom. Stir until combined and cook, stirring, for 2 more minutes. Add the tomato juice and hot pepper paste and bring to the boil. Reduce the heat to low, cover and simmer for 15–20 minutes, until the liquid has been absorbed. Increase the heat to medium and evenly drizzle the remaining 45ml oil around the edges of the rice so it falls to the bottom of the frying pan. Use a spatula to press the rice down repeatedly for about 5 minutes, until the rice on the underside is browned. Remove from the heat.

To serve, place a large round plate on top of the frying pan. Using a heavy towel and holding the plate and pan together, flip the frying pan onto the plate so that the crusted rice from the bottom of the frying pan is on top. Serve immediately.

CORIANDER GREEN BEANS
WITH TOASTED ALMONDS

The popularity of this dish has always surprised me, as I was not expecting adulation for such a humble vegetable. Many of us think of green beans as a bland, soggy, afterthought to our traditional roast dinner plates. But this, my friends, is most certainly not that. These toothsome green beans are flash-fried to give them a slight caramelisation, then they are tossed with coriander to lend them an intriguing, aromatic, almost floral quality and adorned with crunchy roasted almonds. I serve them at my family Thanksgiving every November (no one misses the mushroom soup and tinned fried onions) and alongside roasted chicken throughout the year.

Although ground coriander is the seed of the fresh coriander herb, the two taste very different. So if you don't care for coriander, don't worry, you will still love these green beans. **MAKES 6–8 SERVINGS**

Vegetable oil, for frying
80g flaked almonds
900g fresh green beans, topped and tailed
    and halved crossways
120ml olive oil
6 cloves garlic, chopped
2 tablespoons ground coriander
1 tablespoon freshly ground black pepper
Sea salt
Lemon wedges

Roasting and Toasting

If you don't feel like frying, instead toss the beans with 120ml olive oil and roast them in a single layer on a baking tray in a 260°C/gas mark 10 oven, until tender and blistered, 15–20 minutes. The nuts can be toasted in a dry pan set over a medium heat until golden and fragrant, about 5 minutes.

Fill a deep frying pan halfway with vegetable oil and set it over a medium heat. When it's hot but not smoking, add the almonds and fry until just golden and fragrant, about 1 minute. Using a slotted spoon, remove them to a kitchen paper–lined plate.

Working in two or three batches, add the green beans to the oil and fry until tender and browned, 3–5 minutes. Remove the green beans with a slotted spoon, drain on a kitchen paper–lined plate, then transfer to a serving plate.

Empty the frying oil from the frying pan and add the olive oil. Heat over a medium heat, add the garlic and cook until golden brown, about 2 minutes. Add the coriander and black pepper and season with salt; cook until you smell the coriander toasting, about 1 minute. Turn the heat off, add the reserved almonds and stir to combine. Sprinkle over the green beans and serve with lemon wedges.

SAUTÉED HEARTS OF COURGETTE

NA'IR

Na'ir translates to 'pulp' in Arabic (in this case, squash pulp), and it has a long and storied tradition from my childhood in Nazareth. When I was growing up, my mum, a schoolteacher and mother of five, would always prepare meals ahead of time. Weekend suppers would be readied on Thursdays and cooked on Saturdays, and one of those meals was the delectable mashi: stuffed squash and aubergine. This left her with a pile of squash pulp (she discarded the aubergine pulp, as it was too bitter), which she would use to make a few extra meals. On Friday mornings, we had eggs and na'ir formed into a squash fritter or sautéed with olive oil, caramelised onions and pickled chillies, and served as a generous side dish for the mashi on Saturday.

In keeping with my mother's sense of economy, be sure to use up the hollowed-out courgette shells in other dishes, such as Quinoa Pilaf (page 84), Squash with Chickpeas in Minted Yogurt (page 92), or Grilled Sweetcorn Salad (page 82). You could also swap them for the turnips in Freekeh Stuffed Turnips in Tamarind Sauce (page 112). **MAKES 4–6 SERVINGS**

15 large courgettes

Sea salt

120ml olive oil

1 medium onion, chopped

1 large shallot, chopped

1 poblano or long hot chilli, finely chopped

1 tablespoon ground allspice

1 teaspoon freshly ground black pepper

½ teaspoon ground cumin

Pinch of freshly grated nutmeg

Pinch of ground cinnamon

Yogurt, hot bread, and olives, for serving

Slice the courgettes in half lengthways. Using a teaspoon, scrape the pulp out of the centres and place it in a colander set over a bowl. Lightly sprinkle the pulp with salt and allow it to sit for 10–15 minutes. Wrap the pulp in a towel and squeeze over the sink, until all the excess moisture has been removed.

Remove excess water from the courgette pulp by sprinkling it with salt and squeezing it inside a tea towel.

In a large frying pan, heat the oil over a medium heat. Add the onions and shallots and cook until golden, about 4 minutes. Add the chilli, allspice, black pepper, cumin, nutmeg and cinnamon. Cook for 1 minute, or until fragrant. Add the courgettes and stir to combine well. Reduce the heat, add 1 teaspoon salt, and cook for 15 minutes, or until very tender. Serve with accompaniments like yogurt, hot bread and olives.

MAIN DISHES

A JOURNEY BEYOND GALILEE

Growing up in the Galilee, we only learned to cook from our mothers and aunts, as typically most meals were made at home seven days a week. It was all a bit of theatre, especially with bigger families. Even more so on the weekends, when big, gregarious dinner parties involving extended family and friends were held. The dinners were done buffet-style, with platters covering every surface, from the kitchen and dining areas straight into the sitting room.

As I came into my own and moved out of my parents' home, I spent a good part of my time in the kitchen trying to be as good a cook as my mother was. I didn't even realise I was any good until someone very dear to me said I'd made a dish even better than my mother. It was an emotional moment — and one that gave me the confidence to continue striving to live up to her standards, but to start adding my own influence to my cooking. The moment I made that decision, everything at Tanoreen changed. That's when I started to colour outside the lines.

In the Big Apple, a different culture is only a subway ride away, which means I can find ingredients from every corner of the globe and work with them in my kitchen as I realise my new vision for Tanoreen. In fact, it was only in New York that I became exposed to food from other Levantine countries. Growing up, I never had the opportunity to go to Syria or Lebanon, but in New York I've explored Syrian grocers and have discovered that they use much the same pantry as I do. My staff and newfound friends come from Lebanon, Egypt, and beyond and they've cooked for me and inspired recipes such as Koshari (page 116), Makdous (page 109), and Aleppo-Style Kibbeh Stew with Carrots (page 146).

That said, I've also been heavily inspired by cultures and ingredients not native to my region of the world, and that's equally what this book is about. So while Sweet & Sour Soup (page 125), Chicken and Aubergine Rollatini (page 138), and Sesame Prawns (page 168) may seem a far cry from Arabic food, I encourage you to look closer, as you will see the indelible influence of the Middle East interwoven throughout.

PORTOBELLO SHAWARMA

This recipe has been in the making for fifty years. While that might sound dramatic, it's a perfect example of the role food memories can play in inspiring creative new uses for familiar ingredients. When I was growing up, my father, Anton, loved to forage for wild vegetables, herbs and fruit. He would pick all sorts of mushrooms and teach us how to distinguish between the edible and poisonous varieties. He also tried (with no success at the time) to convince us that the heartier mushrooms could be used instead of meat in customary dishes that my mother made. Eventually, as an adult, I came around to the idea, and my daughter, Jumana, did, too, when I came up with this vegan portobello shawarma. It's as spicy and satisfying as the original and will please even the most committed carnivore.

MAKES 4–6 LARGE PITTA SANDWICHES

900g portobello or baby portobello mushrooms, stems removed and caps finely chopped

1 teaspoon mild curry powder

1 teaspoon freshly ground black pepper

1 teaspoon ground coriander

1 teaspoon ground cumin

1 teaspoon ground turmeric

½ teaspoon ground cardamom

¼ teaspoon freshly grated nutmeg

3 cloves garlic, diced

6 tablespoons olive oil

6 tablespoons distilled white vinegar

Sea salt

Pitta bread, cucumbers, tomatoes, pickles, Harissa (page 212) and Tahini Yogurt Sauce (page 209), for serving

In a large bowl, combine all the ingredients except the salt and serving options. Toss well to coat the mushrooms. Heat a large frying pan over a medium heat, add the mushroom mixture, and cook for 4–6 minutes, stirring occasionally, until the mushrooms are tender. Season with salt and pile into pittas along with whatever toppings you like, to make sandwiches.

NOTE: Set up a shawarma bar for a party with warm pittas, chopped red onion, chopped parsley, pickles, tahini and harissa so each guest can build his or her own sandwich.

AN EXCUSE FOR KIBBEH

Before it became trendy, my family followed what would be called a Mediterranean diet, mostly out of necessity. We pressed our own olive oil, planted vegetables and fruit trees and used fresh goat's milk for yogurt. Our diets were heavily vegetarian and the food was organic. My grandmother used to make kibbeh t'heeleh when we'd visit her village, and the whole family would gather – sometimes up to thirty of us! Having that many mouths to feed made it especially difficult to afford meat, which few house-holds enjoyed more than once a week. No wonder everyone seemed to have a version of this inexpensive, lamb-free 'excuse' for kibbeh, formed from whatever they had on hand and often served with homemade yogurt.

 As for my variation, I've never been a big fan of dairy (except cheese!), so I skipped the base of yogurt and used lentils instead, and shaped the kibbeh from potatoes because I knew they'd stay firm in the stew. I wanted to make this dish completely vegan but still hearty enough for a meat eater to appreciate.

MAKES 8–10 SERVINGS

BULGAR DOUGH

450g fine bulgar wheat

2 large starchy potatoes, peeled, cut into
 6 pieces each

Sea salt

2 shallots

2 tablespoons Hot Pepper Paste (page 212) or Harissa
 (page 212)

1½ tablespoons Tanoreen Kibbeh Spice Mix

or

 1 teaspoon ground cumin

 1 teaspoon freshly ground black pepper

 1 teaspoon ground allspice

 ¼ teaspoon freshly grated nutmeg

 ½ teaspoon ground marjoram

STUFFING

60ml olive oil

1 red onion, finely diced

4 shallots, finely diced

10g chopped fresh coriander

40g flaked almonds

3 tablespoons sumac

½ teaspoon sea salt

LENTIL STEW

60ml olive oil

1 white onion, diced

3 shallots, diced

1 teaspoon ground cumin

1 teaspoon freshly ground black pepper

1 tablespoon ground coriander

1 tablespoon sea salt

1 poblano or jalapeño chilli, diced

25g chopped fresh coriander

8 cloves garlic, diced

450g red lentils

2 tablespoons Hot Pepper Paste (page 212; optional)

Juice of 1 lemon

Chopped fresh coriander, Harissa (page 212), and
 fresh lemon juice, for serving

(CONTINUED)

Make the dough: Pour the bulgar into a bowl, add water to barely cover, and set aside to soak for 30 minutes. All of the water should be absorbed, but if not, drain any excess away. Put the potatoes in a medium saucepan with salted water to cover. Bring to the boil over a medium heat, cook until they are easily pierced with a knife and then drain.

In a food processor, combine the soaked bulgar, potatoes, shallots, hot pepper paste, if using and spice mix and season with salt. Process until a sticky dough is formed.

Make the stuffing: In a medium frying pan, heat the oil over a medium heat. Add the onion and shallots and cook until golden brown, about 4 minutes. Add the coriander, almonds, sumac and salt. Stir to combine and turn off the heat.

Prepare a bowl of ice water. Moisten your hands with the water and form the kibbeh by rolling the dough into 4–5cm balls. Flatten slightly in your palms and add ½ teaspoon of the stuffing to the centres. Close the dough around it, roll the dough between your palms to make balls, then flatten the balls slightly. If you're feeling fancy, you can also use your fingers to pinch the tops of the balls to create droplet shapes (as shown opposite).

To fry the kibbeh, pour enough vegetable oil into a large pan or deep fryer so that the kibbeh will be submerged. Heat until hot but not smoking. Fry the kibbeh until golden brown. Alternatively, you may bake the kibbeh: Liberally brush the kibbeh with oil, place on a baking tray, and bake in a 200°C/gas mark 6 oven for 20–30 minutes, until the kibbeh are crisp on the outside.

Make the lentil stew: Heat the oil in a large, deep saucepan over a medium heat. Add the onion and shallots and cook for 3 minutes, until softened. Add the cumin, black pepper, coriander and salt. Add the chilli, cook for another 3 minutes, then add the garlic and cook until the vegetables are softened and lightly browned. Add the coriander, lentils and 1.4 litres water. Bring to a simmer and cook, uncovered, until the lentils are very tender, about 20 minutes. Add the hot pepper paste and lemon juice.

To serve: Divide the lentils among shallow soup bowls. Top with the kibbeh, coriander and additional harissa or lemon juice, if desired.

NOTE: Want to make your life even easier? The kibbeh can be rolled and enjoyed without the stuffing. Care to prep in advance? Uncooked kibbeh balls can be stored in the freezer for up to a month, but don't defrost them before cooking, as they will become soggy. They can go directly from freezer to fryer (carefully).

TOP: Hold a slightly flattened ball of kibbeh in one hand and use the index finger of the other hand to form a depression in the middle of the ball; spoon in the stuffing.
BOTTOM: Pinch the dough closed around the stuffing; pinch the top of the closed kibbie into a droplet shape if you like.

STUFFED AUBERGINE OVER TOASTED PITTA

MAKDOUS FETTI

There's a restaurant in Jordan called the Fetti Place, which, as you would expect, serves all kinds of fetti (a dish of meat layered with toasted pitta, rice pilaf, and yogurt sauce). It's where I first discovered makdous fetti, although it was filled with lamb rather than pickled aubergine stuffed with walnuts (as the name would suggest). When I came home, I was determined to make my own version that was full of flavour but completely vegetarian. Don't feel like going full fetti? You can simply serve the stuffed aubergine over plain rice for a wonderful meat-free meal. Want to condense the recipe still further? Instead of making your own tomato sauce, swap 480ml shop-bought sauce and stir in 4 tablespoons of pomegranate molasses. **MAKES 6 SERVINGS**

AUBERGINE

12 baby aubergines

1 teaspoon sea salt, plus more for salting the aubergines

120ml olive oil, plus for more frying or roasting

3 shallots, finely diced

3 cloves garlic, finely chopped

1 long hot or poblano chilli, finely diced

10g chopped fresh coriander

12g fresh basil leaves

1 teaspoon ground cumin

1 teaspoon freshly ground black pepper

1 teaspoon ground allspice

1 teaspoon ground coriander

Pinch of freshly grated nutmeg (optional)

Pinch of ground cardamom (optional)

12 Arabic squash or yellow squash, or 6 small courgettes, chopped

6 plum tomatoes, chopped

480ml Spicy Tomato Sauce (page 213)

6 (20cm) pitta breads, toasted

Tahini Yogurt Sauce (page 209)

Rice and Vermicelli Pilaf (page 140)

80g flaked almonds, toasted

Prepare the aubergines: Preheat the oven to 260°C/gas mark 10 . Partially peel the aubergines in alternating lengthways stripes, leaving the crowns intact. Sprinkle with salt and place in a colander to sweat for 15–20 minutes. Pat dry with kitchen paper. Brush with the olive oil and roast for about 25 minutes. Alternatively, heat the oil in a large frying pan over medium heat, and shallow-fry the aubergine until golden, about 5 minutes.

Heat 60ml of the olive oil in a large sauté pan. Add the shallots and cook for about 3 minutes, until tender. Add the garlic, chilli, coriander and basil and cook until the herbs are wilted. Add the cumin, black pepper, allspice, coriander, nutmeg and cardamom, if using, and cook until fragrant, about 2 minutes. Add the remaining 60ml oil and the squash, cover the pan, and cook for 8–10 minutes, until tender.

(CONTINUED)

Add the tomatoes and salt, cover again, and cook for 3 minutes. Meanwhile, lower the oven temperature to 180°C/gas mark 4.

Make a deep lengthways slit in each aubergine, being careful not to cut through the bottom. Stuff 2–3 tablespoons of the vegetable filling into each cavity and arrange in a single layer in a large casserole dish or rimmed baking tray. Pour the tomato sauce over the top, cover with foil and bake for 15 minutes.

Assemble the fetti: Arrange the toasted pitta bread on the bottom of a platter. Drizzle with one-third of the tomato sauce from the pan and some of the yogurt sauce. Cover with rice and vermicelli pilaf, followed by another drizzle of tomato sauce and yogurt sauce. Top with the aubergine, the remaining tomato sauce and yogurt sauce and the toasted almonds and serve.

The Versatility of Aubergine

Aubergine is one of the cornerstones of Middle Eastern cooking and also one of the most versatile and cross-cultural of ingredients. It is stuffed, fried, made into spreads, tossed into salads, cured in olive oil and even used as a dessert.

I call aubergine a flavor sponge, as it adapts perfectly to countless applications in the kitchen. On the other hand, aubergine's structure also means it can soak up a lot of oil when fried. To avoid this, just make sure the oil is kept very hot when frying; this will quickly seal the exposed surface, preventing the oil from seeping all the way through. (Remember when it comes to frying, you always want an oil that can withstand high heat, such as canola, grapeseed or vegetable.)

I always follow a traditional technique that achieves three goals: It reduces the aubergine from absorbing too much oil when frying, really concentrates the flavor, and simultaneously removes bitterness. Place the peeled and sliced or diced aubergine into a colander that has been lined with paper towels. Sprinkle with salt, set it over a large bowl, and let sit for an hour. The excess liquid will drain away. Rinse the aubergine and pat dry before cooking.

CAULIFLOWER TAHINI TAGINE

This was my father's favourite dish, and he taught me how to make it many years ago. Then, when I got married, guess which dish my husband knew how to make best? Cauliflower tahini tagine! We've made both for dinner parties and competed, challenging our guests to choose the best version. Truth be told, his was quite good, but, he was gracious in defeat. Admired by carnivores, vegans and vegetarians alike, my competition-winning tagine has a rich, stick-to-your bones heartiness thanks to flash-fried florets and sticky, pomegranate molasses–sweetened tahini. With all due respect to my husband, I think it will win you over too. **MAKES 4–6 SERVINGS**

CAULIFLOWER

60ml olive oil

4 medium shallots, thinly sliced

Vegetable oil, for roasting or frying

2 medium heads cauliflower, trimmed and broken into florets

TAHINI SAUCE

450g tahini

240ml fresh lemon juice

2 tablespoons Hot Pepper Paste (page 212 or shop-bought, optional)

4 tablespoons pomegranate molasses

10g chopped fresh coriander

6 cloves garlic, crushed

1 tablespoon sea salt, or to taste

1 teaspoon ground cumin

1 teaspoon freshly ground black pepper

1 teaspoon ground coriander

½ teaspoon ground allspice

Arabic bread or Rice and Vermicelli Pilaf (page 140), for serving

Make the cauliflower: Heat the olive oil in a small frying pan over a medium heat, add the shallots and cook until golden brown, 4–6 minutes. Remove from the heat and set aside.

Fill a large frying pan with vegetable oil to a depth of 4cm. Heat over a medium heat until hot, but not smoking. Add the cauliflower in batches and fry until golden brown, about 5 minutes. (Alternatively, brush the florets with vegetable oil or olive oil and roast in a 200°C/gas mark 6 oven until golden brown, about 20 minutes.)

Make the tahini sauce: Combine all of the tahini sauce ingredients in a blender, add 240ml water and blend until smooth. Taste and add more salt if needed.

Preheat the oven to 200°C/gas mark 6. Place the fried or roasted cauliflower florets in a large, deep baking dish and cover with the tahini sauce. Scatter the shallots over the top. Using a large spoon, gently fold the ingredients together once or twice to combine. Cover the pan with aluminium foil and bake for 40 minutes. Uncover and bake for another 5 minutes, or until browned on top. Serve with Arabic bread or Rice and Vermicelli Pilaf.

FREEKEH-STUFFED TURNIPS
WITH TAMARIND SAUCE

The culture of *mashi* ('stuffed' in Arabic) crosses all borders in the Middle East, as it's found in every region. Spiced lamb and rice pressed into hollowed-out vegetables is comfort in a pan for millions of Middle Easterners. Yet this dish demonstrates that you can utilise an entirely different collection of ingredients while still remaining faithful to tradition. Toasty freekeh ably stands in for the lamb here, creamy turnips form the ideal edible bowl, and a sauce of potent tamarind adds just the right touch of tartness. This dish is freekishly good . . . sorry, I couldn't resist. **MAKES 8 SERVINGS**

VEGETABLES

8 large turnips, peeled

8 large carrots

Fresh lime juice

STUFFING

120ml olive oil

2 shallots, diced

1 long hot chilli, diced (optional)

3 cloves garlic, chopped

15g chopped fresh flat-leaf parsley

1½ teaspoons ground cumin

1 teaspoon freshly ground black pepper

2 tablespoons Tanoreen Spice Mix
    or
    2 tablespoons ground allspice
    1 teaspoon ground coriander
    ½ teaspoon freshly grated nutmeg
    ½ teaspoon ground cardamom
    ¼ teaspoon ground ginger

4–6 food-grade dried rosebuds (optional)

1 tablespoon sea salt, plus more for finishing

600g freekeh

2.1 litres water or vegetable stock

TAMARIND SAUCE

220g tamarind pulp with seeds

1 tablespoon Hot Pepper Paste (page 212, or
    shop-bought)

Prepare the turnips and carrots: Evenly hollow out the insides of the turnips with an apple corer or paring knife, leaving about 1.25cm of flesh around the sides. Sprinkle the turnips and carrots with lime juice so they don't discolour and set aside.

Make the stuffing: Heat the oil in a large saucepan over a medium heat. Add the shallots and cook until golden, about 4 minutes. Add the chilli, if using, and cook until softened, about 2 minutes. Add the garlic and cook until aromatic, about 30 seconds. Add the parsley, cumin, black pepper, Tanoreen spices, rosebuds (if using) and salt and stir to combine.

Add the freekeh and water or vegetable stock, bring to the boil, then reduce the heat to low, cover and simmer until the freekeh is tender and the liquid has been absorbed, 15–20 minutes. Turn the heat off and let sit in the pan for about 5 minutes, then spread over a baking tray to cool.

Preheat the oven to 200°C/gas mark 6.

Make the tamarind sauce: In a medium bowl, whisk the tamarind pulp with 480ml hot water. Pour the mixture into a fine-mesh sieve set over a bowl and push it through to strain it. Take whatever remains in the bowl and place it in a medium saucepan along with 1.9 litres water. Set over a medium heat and cook until it boils and thickens, 10–15 minutes. Add the hot pepper paste, stir to dissolve it, and remove from the heat.

(CONTINUED)

Stuff the turnips with the freekeh stuffing (you will have stuffing left over). Arrange the turnips and carrots on a large baking tray and layer the leftover freekeh on top of them. Cover with the tamarind sauce and cover the pan with aluminium foil.

Place the baking tray in the oven and bake for 30 minutes. Reduce the oven temperature to 180°C/gas mark 4 and bake for another 15 minutes, or until the vegetables are completely tender. Sprinkle with salt, if desired, and serve.

Broad Beans

If you're familiar with broad beans, you might find it odd that this recipe calls for chopping the pods into pieces and stirring them directly into the stew rather than peeling them first. But this is actually a very common practice in the Middle East (and other parts of the world) for dishes that call for young, tender beans. It's the mature, woody specimens that need to be peeled before cooking. Determined to make this dish in the off-season? Prowl Middle Eastern grocery stores, which often carry stashes of frozen young pods.

Tamarind

Tamarind is one of my favourite modern Middle Eastern pantry staples. It's found in Latin American and South Asian markets. Encased in fat, peanut-like pods growing from a tropical tree, this sticky, intoxicating fruit is multiple tastes in one, lending a concentrated sweet-and-sour element to everything it touches. It is commonly used in drinks, chutneys and sweets. I use it in countless ways — as a seasoning for soup, a flavouring for meat-filled potatoes and a sauce for stuffed turnips, to mention a few.

But while versatile, tamarind can be intimidating. Visit a market and you'll likely come across fresh and dried pods, bottles of sweetened syrup, jars of ready-to-use concentrate, and blocks of compressed pulp. My advice? Unless you're seasoned at soaking and cleaning the seeds, bypass the pulp and pods (except for in the above recipe) and zero in on the jars of paste concentrate, which are ready to be whisked into just about anything you choose.

FRESH BROAD BEANS
WITH SPICED YOGURT SAUCE

In the springtime, when emerald green broad beans appear at vegetable markets sporting pods so tender they can be eaten whole, I immediately get to work on this simple minty stew. There's something nostalgic about adjusting my menu to the weather: while I can't make this dish every time I crave it, savouring my first bite of spring broad beans each year is always worth the wait. **MAKES 6–8 SERVINGS**

1.35kg fresh young broad beans in the pod

4 cups natural low-fat yogurt, homemade (page 94) or shop-bought

1 tablespoon cornflour

1 tablespoon sea salt, plus more to taste

165ml olive oil

6 cloves garlic, chopped

1½ teaspoons dried mint

2 large shallots, chopped

1 medium onion, chopped

10g chopped fresh coriander

1½ teaspoons freshly ground white pepper (or 1 tablespoon black pepper)

1 tablespoon ground cumin

1 tablespoon Tanoreen Spice Mix
   or
    1 tablespoon ground allspice
    ½ teaspoon ground coriander
    ¼ teaspoon freshly grated nutmeg
    ¼ teaspoon ground cardamom
    ¼ teaspoon ground ginger

2 or 3 food-grade rosebuds (optional)

Juice of 1 lemon

Fresh mint leaves, for garnish

Arabic bread (such as pitta or Flatbread, page 33) and pickles or rice, for serving

To prepare the broad beans, remove the string running along the length of the pod by bending the tip and pulling down the seam of the pod. Cut the pods crossways into multiple segments by slicing between each individual bean. Wash in a colander and set aside to drain.

Place the yogurt, cornflour and salt in a large saucepan and whisk to combine. Turn the heat to medium and cook, stirring occasionally, until the yogurt begins to thicken and boil, about 10 minutes. Reduce the heat to low.

Meanwhile, heat 3 tablespoons of the oil in a small frying pan over a medium heat. Add 1 tablespoon of the garlic and cook until light golden. Add the dried mint and stir to combine.

Bring the yogurt back to the boil and add the hot mint mixture. Stir to combine, then transfer the yogurt to a large serving bowl.

Heat the remaining 120ml oil in a large sauté pan over a medium heat. Add the shallots and onion and cook for 8–10 minutes, until golden brown. Add the remaining 1 tablespoon garlic and cook for 2 minutes, until fragrant. Add the coriander and cook until it wilts. Add the white pepper, cumin, Tanoreen Spices and rosebuds, if using, and cook for 1 minute. Add the broad beans, reduce the heat to low, cover, and cook until the beans are tender, about 15 minutes.

Add the lemon juice, season with salt and cook for 2 minutes more. Pour the mixture over the yogurt and stir to combine. Serve at room temperature or cold, along with bread and pickles or rice.

EGYPTIAN-STYLE LENTIL & NOODLE PILAF

KOSHARI

I love a culinary challenge. So when my daughter, Jumana, returned from her graduate studies in Egypt, she asked me to make their most popular street food, koshari, widely regarded as the national dish of Egypt. It is also one of the most carbohydrate-dense dishes I have come across, combining two types of pasta and rice. The dish was created for families on a budget with many mouths to feed. But it's also highly satisfying, with two types of lentils providing a great source of vegetarian protein. Not only did my daughter give it top marks, I'm proud to say that it was very well received by my Egyptian customers as well. **MAKES 6–8 SERVINGS**

PASTA AND LENTILS
240ml vegetable oil

4 onions, halved and sliced vertically
    into paper-thin strips

175g brown lentils

450g macaroni

240ml olive oil

2 large shallots, diced

1 long hot or poblano chilli, deseeded and diced

25g chopped fresh coriander

100g vermicelli noodles

185g Egyptian or other short-grain rice

175g red lentils

1 tablespoon freshly ground black pepper

1½ teaspoons ground allspice

1 tablespoon ground cumin

1 tablespoon sea salt

960ml boiling water

HOT SAUCE
2 tablespoons olive oil

6 cloves garlic, crushed

1 long hot or other chilli, deseeded and diced

1 teaspoon ground cumin

½ teaspoon freshly ground black pepper

120ml distilled white vinegar

4 tablespoons Hot Pepper Paste (page 212)

120ml fresh lemon juice

Make the pasta and lentils: Heat the vegetable oil in a deep frying pan over a medium heat until it is very hot, but not smoking. Add the onions and fry until golden brown, stirring every few minutes. Using a slotted spoon, remove one-third of the onions and place them on a kitchen paper–lined plate to drain, and leave the other two-thirds in the pan to get deeply browned and crispy. Remove the remaining onions from the oil to a separate kitchen paper–lined plate. (You can discard the oil, or use it in the recipe in place of some of the olive oil.)

Meanwhile, in a medium saucepan, bring 480ml water to the boil over a high heat. Add the brown lentils and cook for about 15 minutes, until al dente. Drain and set aside. Bring a separate saucepan of water to the boil, add the macaroni, and cook for 8–10 minutes, until al dente. Drain and set aside.

In the pan you fried the onions in, heat 160ml of the olive oil over a medium heat. Add the shallots and chilli and cook for 3 minutes, then add the coriander and cook for another 2 minutes. Add the vermicelli and cook until it is lightly browned, about 4 minutes. Add the rice and cook, stirring, for 2 minutes. Add the cooked brown lentils and uncooked red lentils, the black pepper, allspice, cumin and salt. Add the boiling water, return to the boil, and add the reserved golden brown onions. Cover, reduce the heat to maintain a simmer, and simmer for 15 minutes, or until the water is completely absorbed. Stir in the remaining 80ml olive oil and turn off the heat.

Make the hot sauce: Heat the olive oil in a small frying pan. Add the garlic and chilli and cook until golden brown. Stir in the cumin and black pepper and let sizzle for a few seconds. Reduce the heat and add the vinegar. Bring to the boil and stir in the hot pepper paste. Add the lemon juice and 120ml water, bring to the boil and boil for 3–5 minutes.

Serve on a large platter in layers, starting with the koshari, then half of the crispy onions, then the macaroni, hot sauce and the remaining crispy onions.

CRISPY CAULIFLOWER STEAKS
WITH TAHINI & POMEGRANATE

One day at the restaurant, we got in a shipment of particularly perfect cauliflower from a farm in upstate New York. These cruciferous beauties were so grand that I was compelled to cut them into slabs, coat them in Japanese breadcrumbs, herbs and cheese and pan-fry them until crisp on the outside and tender inside, and that's how this dish was born. **MAKES 4–8 SERVINGS**

COATING

175g unseasoned breadcrumbs (I prefer panko)

1 heaped tablespoon lemon pepper
    (or black pepper mixed with lemon zest)

1 tablespoon dried basil

1 tablespoon dried oregano or za'atar

¼ teaspoon ground ginger

¼ teaspoon garlic powder

1 teaspoon paprika

40g shredded Parmesan cheese

15g finely chopped fresh parsley, or
    1 tablespoon dried parsley

CAULIFLOWER

130g plain flour (or substitute cornmeal)

4 large egg whites, beaten

2 large heads cauliflower

1 teaspoon sea salt

½ teaspoon freshly ground black pepper

Vegetable oil, for frying

Tahini Pomegranate Hot Sauce (page 209)

Make the coating: In a large bowl, combine all the coating ingredients.

Prepare the cauliflower: Put the flour and egg whites into separate shallow bowls. Vertically slice each head of cauliflower into two fat, flat-sided steaks. Save the trimmings for another use such as a stir-fry or vegetable soup stock. Sprinkle the cauliflower steaks with the salt and pepper and coat well with flour. Dip the cauliflower into the egg whites, then the coating mixture, making sure it adheres on all sides.

Pour enough oil into a large frying pan so that it will submerge the cauliflower halfway or into a deep-fat fryer so that it will submerge the cauliflower completely. Heat the oil until very hot, but not smoking. Working in batches, fry the cauliflower for 5–6 minutes on each side, until tender and golden brown, setting each batch on kitchen paper as it is done. Place on a serving platter, drizzle tahini pomegranate hot sauce or lemon juice over the cauliflower, and serve.

While I usually finish my cauliflower steaks with Tahini Pomegranate Hot Sauce, I'm equally happy topping them with a simple squeeze of lemon. Lemon brightens everything it touches, in particular fried or spicy foods. I eat close to three lemons a day, sometimes even five. There's little I love more than the taste of fresh, vivid lemon! Use your judgment—if you prefer your food a little less tart, use less juice than the recipe suggests, but if you're like me, go ahead and squeeze with abandon!

JERUSALEM ARTICHOKE & SAGE SAUTE

The secret to getting vegan and vegetarian dishes to really come alive? Don't shy away from spice and concentrate your efforts on texture. That's why I like to roast Jerusalem artichokes – for a caramelised exterior and supple interior – then sprinkle them with spices for a smoky depth. Basil and sage bring a welcome bit of freshness, and intensely fruity pomegranate juice and its sweet-sour molasses relative bind the flavours together. There is so much going on here, there's simply no opportunity to miss the meat. If you prefer a saucier stew, add another 240ml of pomegranate juice and serve over rice. **MAKES 4–6 SERVINGS**

1.35kg Jerusalem artichokes, peeled (select evenly
    sized ones, about 5cm long)

120ml olive oil, plus more for roasting

2 poblano chillies, chopped

6 cloves garlic, chopped

1 tablespoon freshly ground black pepper

1 tablespoon ground coriander

1½ teaspoons ground cumin

1½ teaspoons chilli flakes

25g chopped fresh basil

2 tablespoons chopped fresh sage, or
    1½ teaspoons dried sage

4 tablespoons pomegranate or grape molasses
    (or the juice of 1½ lemons)

240ml unsweetened pomegranate juice

Sea salt

Arabic bread (such as pitta or Flatbread,
    page 33), for serving

Preheat the oven to 200°C/gas mark 6.

Place the Jerusalem artichokes in a roasting pan, brush with oil and roast until just tender, about 30 minutes. Remove from the oven and set aside to cool.

Heat the oil in a large frying pan over a medium heat. Add the chillies and cook until softened, about 4 minutes. Add the garlic and cook until golden, about 2 minutes. Add the black pepper, coriander, cumin and chilli flakes and cook for 1 minute. Add the basil and sage and cook until wilted, about 1 minute. Add the pomegranate molasses and pomegranate juice and bring to the boil. Add the reserved Jerusalem artichokes, gently stir once to combine and cover. Cook for 5–10 minutes, until the Jerusalem artichokes are softened and the sauce has been mostly absorbed. Season with salt and serve with bread.

So what in the world are Jerusalem artichokes? Also known as sunchokes, they look like a large length of fresh turmeric, a piece of stubby ginger, or an odd, knobby potato. Yet they're not a spice, not a starch and they bear no relation to artichokes (or, for that matter, Jerusalem). These thin-skinned tubers are actually in the sunflower family and are native to North America. They have a crisp, clean, slightly nutty flavour, not unlike water chestnuts. They can be used interchangeably with potatoes (roasted, fried, puréed, or even mashed) but contain no other carbohydrate but inulin – a type of dietary fibre naturally occurring in plants – which makes Jerusalem artichokes an excellent choice for diabetics.

CHICKPEA SOUP
WITH BABY ONIONS

Some soups spring straight out of my imagination, while others are deeply rooted in the flavours I grew up with. The latter is certainly the case with this soup, rich with warming North African spices based on the complex sauce for a dish called *maftoul*, one of Palestine's oldest, most important main dishes. Maftoul consists of couscous studded with chickpeas and served with an intensely flavourful stock on the side for spooning over the top. As kids, we'd always attack that bowl, and my mum would scream at us because there wouldn't be enough left for the rest of the table. I always wondered why that sauce couldn't be turned into soup so there would always be plenty for everyone. So when I set up my own kitchen, that's precisely what I did! **MAKES 8–10 SERVINGS**

120ml olive oil, or 115g butter or ghee

5 shallots or 2 small yellow onions, diced

900g baby onions, peeled

Sea salt

1 tablespoon ground caraway seeds (available online)

1 tablespoon ground cumin

1 teaspoon freshly ground black pepper

1 tablespoon Tanoreen Spice Mix

or

   1½ teaspoons ground allspice

   1 teaspoon ground cardamom

   1 teaspoon ground cinnamon

   1 tablespoon ground coriander

   Pinch of freshly grated nutmeg

450g dried chickpeas, soaked and simmered until tender (or 4 x 400g tins, drained and rinsed)

2.25 litres vegetable stock

Juice of 1 lemon

Heat the oil in a soup pan over a medium heat. Add the shallots and cook for about 4 minutes, until translucent. Add the baby onions and cook until they get a bit of colour, 6–8 minutes. Reduce the heat to medium-low, sprinkle with salt, and cook until the baby onions begin to soften, 15–20 minutes. Add the caraway, cumin, black pepper, and Tanoreen Spices and cook for about 2 minutes, until fragrant. Add the chickpeas and stock, bring to the boil, then reduce the heat to medium and cook until the onions are very soft. Season with salt, sprinkle the lemon juice over the top, and serve.

TIP: To revive the taste of tinned chickpeas, heat them in a pan for at least 30 minutes first, adding water as needed so they don't dry out.

In Praise of the Chickpea. I may have omitted them from my houmous recipes in favor of pure, concentrated vegetable flavour, but that in no way diminishes how I feel about chickpeas. Whether tossed with squash and yogurt as a cooling springtime side dish or folded with a velvety slump of onions into a sustaining winter soup, nourishing, inexpensive chickpeas bring so much to the table. So there's no need to fulfill a personal chickpea quota with houmous when it's possible to appreciate chickpeas in so many other ways.

BAKED PUMPKIN KIBBEH

Why should pumpkin be relegated to pie or other trendy fall-flavoured items? Especially when it's such a great addition to savoury dishes, not least kibbeh. Combined with bulgar, pumpkin forms a perfectly mouldable (yet appealingly delicate) shell. And it sandwiches stuffings that are nothing less than a textural dream; think velvety green spinach, crunchy roasted nuts and creamy chickpeas seasoned with sumac. This dish can be prepared in advance and freezes beautifully, making it an equally good choice for an elegant Sunday supper or a rushed weekday meal. It can be eaten warm out of the oven, but is just as tasty at room temperature, so family members on different schedules can enjoy it whenever they get home. **MAKES 10–12 SERVINGS**

OUTER LAYER

340g extra-fine bulgar wheat, soaked in cold water to cover for 30 minutes

450g fresh or tinned pumpkin purée (not pumpkin pie mix)

½ onion, puréed into liquid using a food processor

4 tablespoons plain flour

20g unseasoned breadcrumbs

1 tablespoon Hot Pepper Paste (page 212)

1½ tablespoons Tanoreen Kibbeh Spice Mix

or

    1 tablespoon ground allspice

    1½ teaspoons freshly ground black pepper

    ½ teaspoon ground cumin

    ¼ teaspoon ground cardamom

    ¼ teaspoon freshly grated nutmeg

    ½ teaspoon dried marjoram

Sea salt

STUFFING

2 tablespoons olive oil

250g baby spinach leaves

115g diced onion

70g diced shallots (or additional onion)

140g cooked chickpeas, fresh or tinned

105g coarsely chopped walnuts

10g chopped fresh coriander

2 tablespoons pomegranate molasses

Juice of 1 lemon

1 tablespoon sumac

½ teaspoon ground cumin

½ teaspoon freshly ground black pepper

½ teaspoon ground allspice

Pinch of freshly grated nutmeg

Pinch of chilli flakes (optional)

Sea salt

120ml olive oil, for greasing and brushing

Make the outer layer: In a large bowl, combine the soaked bulgar, pumpkin, puréed onion, flour, breadcrumbs, hot pepper paste and the kibbeh spice mix and season with salt. Dip your hands in a bowl of ice water to keep them moist and mix until the mixture has a workable dough texture that holds its shape when pressed. Divide into two equal pieces.

Make the stuffing: Heat 2 tablespoons of the oil in a large frying pan over a medium heat. Add the spinach leaves and cook, stirring once or twice, until they just begin to wilt, about 2 minutes. Pour the spinach into a colander and use your hands to squeeze any excess liquid out.

(CONTINUED)

Place the spinach in a large bowl and add the remaining stuffing ingredients. Stir well to combine.

Make the kibbeh: Preheat the oven to 200°C/gas mark 6. Grease a 23 x 33cm baking pan with 60ml of the oil.

Take half the kibbeh shell and roll it into a ball. Place the ball in the middle of the pan and start spreading it with your hands (dipping them into the ice water as needed), until the mixture evenly covers the bottom of the pan and partially up the sides. Spread the spinach stuffing in an even layer on top of the kibbeh shell.

Pinch off pieces of the remaining kibbeh shell dough and roll them into balls. Pat the balls into about 1.25cm thickness (remember to keep your hands moist) and evenly distribute them on top of the stuffing. Use your wet fingers to close the gaps between the dough so there is an even, flat layer of kibbeh shell on top of the stuffing.

Brush the kibbeh with the remaining 60ml oil and score into triangles, rectangles, or squares, cutting only through the top layer of the shell. Bake for 20 minutes, then reduce the oven temperature to 120°C/gas ½ and bake for 15 more minutes, or until golden brown. Cut along the scored lines to serve.

The Many Faces of Kibbeh

Another kibbeh recipe, you ask? How many does one need? If you ask a Middle Eastern family, the number is infinite. Translated to 'ball' from the Arabic and classically composed of finely diced lamb and bulgar wheat, kibbeh is the national dish of Lebanon, where you'll find it fried, baked or raw. You'll also find it in Syria — in fact, there are more than seventeen variations in Aleppo alone! Formed into discs or crusted in rice, it's a cherished staple in Iraq, and in Israel it appears as a type of dumpling in soup. My native Palestine is home to the signature ruby-ball shaped kibbeh, tapered shells that are stuffed and deep-fried. So you see, there's much more to kibbeh than a mix of minced meat and wheat.

Kibbeh's adaptability is perfectly suited to how we eat today, which is why I have a chicken option for those who don't eat red meat, fish for pescatarians, and two unique versions that are entirely vegan. And I haven't ruled out the possibility of a gluten-free version. Keeping an international pantry opens up worlds of possibilities for kibbeh. I may have found a subject for my next book!

RAWIA'S SWEET & SOUR SOUP

While it's a wonderful way to warm up during the fall and winter months, soup served a dual purpose in our house. It was a way to make use of a mismatched variety of vegetables left over from the week's cooking. Added to steaming stock and simmered, the odds and ends were magically transformed. Granted, some soups are long and involved to make (better suited for the weekend), but this is a real quick cooker, featuring cabbage, peas, and sprouts, which soften up in minutes. You might think that this soup skews Asian due to its name, but I'm actually referring to my two favourites – pomegranate and tamarind! As each ingredient already contains elements of yin and yang (sweet and sour), this soup achieves a beautiful balance of both. **MAKES 8–10 SERVINGS**

120ml olive oil

3 shallots, diced

1 long hot or poblano chilli, diced (optional)

1 tablespoon chopped garlic

180g shredded white cabbage

155g fresh or frozen baby peas

55g bean sprouts

2 tablespoons Hot Pepper Paste (page 212) or Harissa (page 212)

25g fresh basil leaves, or 4 tablespoons Coriander-Basil Pesto (page 216)

1 teaspoon ground caraway seeds (available online)

1½ teaspoons freshly ground black pepper

Sea salt

480ml tomato juice, preferably fresh

480ml unsweetened tamarind juice

480ml unsweetened pomegranate juice

480ml vegetable or chicken stock

Heat the oil in a large saucepan over a medium heat. Add the shallots and cook until softened, about 5 minutes. Add the chilli, if using, and cook for a few minutes, until softened. Add the garlic and cook until aromatic, about 1 minute. Add the cabbage, peas and bean sprouts and cook until the cabbage starts to wilt, about 8 minutes. Stir in the pepper paste, basil, caraway and black pepper and season with salt. Cook for a few minutes, until fragrant. Add the tomato juice, tamarind juice, pomegranate juice and stock and bring to the boil. Reduce the heat and cook until the cabbage is softened. Taste, adjust the seasonings, spoon into bowls and serve.

JERUSALEM ARTICHOKE & SWEET POTATO SOUP

Ever since I can remember, I've been inventing soups — beyond the vegetable, lentil, chicken or freekeh that I grew up with. Whenever my dad would bring home unexpected vegetables such as kohlrabi and fennel, I'd throw them in a pan and come up with a new soup. It ended up paving the way for a lifelong soup obsession and allowed me to come up with entirely new dishes like this. **MAKES 8–10 SERVINGS**

SOUP

120ml olive oil

4 shallots, chopped

35g chopped spring onions, white parts only

1 sprig rosemary

1 sprig sage

450g Jerusalem artichokes, peeled and cut into 2.5cm pieces

450g sweet potatoes, peeled and cut into 2.5cm pieces

450g carrots, cut into 2.5cm pieces

2–2.5 litres vegetable stock

TEKLAI

75ml olive oil

1 tablespoon diced garlic

1 poblano chilli, finely chopped

25g chopped fresh coriander

1 teaspoon freshly ground black pepper

Sea salt

1½ teaspoons ground cumin

Juice of 1 lemon, or 3 tablespoons pomegranate or grape molasses

1 teaspoon chilli flakes (optional)

Make the soup: Heat the oil in a large saucepan over a medium heat. Add the shallots and cook until lightly browned, 5–7 minutes. Add the spring onions and cook for 2 minutes, then add the rosemary and sage and cook for about 1 minute, until aromatic. Add the Jerusalem artichokes, sweet potatoes and carrots, reduce the heat to very low and cook until the vegetables are softened, 20–25 minutes. Add the stock, increase the heat to medium-high, bring to the boil and season with salt.

While the stock is coming to the boil, make the teklai: Heat the oil in a small saucepan over a medium heat. Add the garlic and chilli and cook until browned, about 4 minutes. Add the coriander and cook until wilted. Add the black pepper, salt to taste, the cumin, lemon juice and chilli flakes, if using. Stir to combine, then immediately pour the teklai over the top of the soup. Spoon into bowls and serve.

NOTE: This recipe is endlessly adaptable. While I love the intense earthiness of Jerusalem artichokes and the natural sweetness of sweet potatoes, you can swap whatever root vegetables or tubers you like. And you can divide the recipe in half if you're feeding just a few people instead of a crowd, but because soup freezes so wonderfully, I never worry about having extra to hand.

FREEKEH & SHIITAKE SOUP

From Chinese wonton to Italian minestrone to Mexican posole, every country has soups that they're associated with, and freekeh soup is one of ours.

The end of summer is when farmers finish harvesting their wheat and smoke it so it can be stored in pantries to keep people fed throughout the winter. When boiled with chicken or lamb and maybe paired with a piece of toasted bread, it's a meal in itself, making freekeh soup a staple of households of all sizes and incomes throughout the Middle East.

Since freekeh actually contains a good deal of protein, I decided it was about time I came up with a version that wasn't dependent on meat. I tried all sorts of vegetables, and unsurprisingly, mushrooms worked the best. While you can use less expensive varieties like button or baby portabellos, shiitakes have a wild smokiness that really complements the nutty green grains. Use the finely milled variety of freekeh for soup if you can find it. **MAKES 8–10 SERVINGS**

120ml olive oil

3 shallots or 1 yellow onion, diced

3 cloves garlic, crushed

1 tablespoon freshly ground black pepper

Pinch of freshly grated nutmeg

½ teaspoon ground allspice

½ teaspoon ground cumin

2.5cm piece of fresh ginger, peeled and grated, or 1 teaspoon ground ginger

450g shiitake mushrooms, cleaned and stems removed

225g finely milled freekeh

2–2.5 litres chicken or vegetable stock

Sea salt

Juice of 1 lemon

Shredded Parmesan cheese or chopped fresh flat-leaf parsley, for garnish

Lemon wedges

Heat the oil in a large saucepan over a medium heat. Add the shallots and cook until golden brown, about 6 minutes. Add the garlic and cook until fragrant, about 3 more minutes. Add the black pepper, nutmeg, allspice, cumin, and ginger and stir to combine. Add the mushrooms, increase the heat to high, and cook until the mushrooms are softened, 5–7 minutes.

Using a slotted spoon (so you remove as little of the spice mix and oil from the pan as possible), transfer the mushrooms to a bowl. Add the freekeh and stock and bring to the boil. Boil for 10–15 minutes, until the freekeh is tender, but not mushy. Return the mushrooms to the pan, boil for 2 minutes, then turn the heat off and season with salt. Spoon into bowls, squeeze the lemon juice over the top, and serve sprinkled with cheese or parsley and with lemon wedges alongside.

BUTTERNUT SQUASH NAPOLEONS

These napoleons perfectly illustrate the expression 'you eat with your eyes first'. While flavour is always my top priority, presentation is essential, especially at the restaurant. This dish, a savoury take on the classic French dessert of layered puff pastry and custard, is an exercise in contrast — in texture and temperature, yes, but also between cultures. Spicy ginger and herbaceous za'atar perfume the Japanese breadcrumbs that crust wheels of earthy, hot-from-the-fryer butternut squash, cradling cool layers of tahini and roasted vegetable–enriched houmous. **MAKES 8 SERVINGS**

2 large butternut squash, peeled, cut into 2.5cm-thick rounds, seeds removed

4 tablespoons olive oil

1 tablespoon freshly ground black pepper

1 tablespoon sea salt

1 teaspoon ground cumin

COATING

175g panko breadcrumbs

1 heaped tablespoon lemon pepper (or black pepper mixed with lemon zest)

1 tablespoon dried basil

1 tablespoon dried oregano or za'atar

¼ teaspoon ground ginger

¼ teaspoon garlic powder

1 teaspoon paprika

130g plain flour (can use gluten-free or cornmeal)

4 large egg whites, beaten

40g shredded Parmesan cheese

15g finely chopped fresh parsley, or 1 tablespoon dried parsley

Vegetable oil, for frying

Roasted Beetroot or Butternut Squash Houmous (page 42) or shop-bought houmous of your choice and Tahini Pomegranate Hot Sauce (page 209), for serving

Preheat the oven to 260°C/gas mark 10.

Drizzle the squash slices with 1 teaspoon of the olive oil each, followed by an even sprinkling of the pepper, salt and cumin. Rub to coat well on all sides. Place on a baking tray and roast for 12–15 minutes, until just tender but not browned. Set aside to cool.

Make the breading: In a shallow bowl, toss the breadcrumbs with the lemon pepper, basil, oregano, ginger, garlic powder and paprika. Pour the flour into a second shallow bowl and beat the egg whites in a third shallow bowl. Dip the squash slices in the flour and turn to evenly coat, then dip them in the egg white. Finish by coating the squash with the seasoned breadcrumbs, making sure they adhere on all sides.

Fill a large frying pan with vegetable oil to a depth of 1.25cm, or fill a deep-fat fryer to a depth that will fully submerge the squash slices. Heat until very hot, but not smoking. Working in batches, fry the squash for 3 minutes on each side, until softened and golden brown all over. Using a slotted spoon, remove the squash from the oil and set on kitchen paper to drain.

Alternatively, to bake instead of frying, lightly coat the breadcrumb crust with cooking spray or oil, and cook in a 190°C/gas mark 5 oven until golden and tender, about 30 minutes.

Assemble the napoleons: Top one squash slice with a generous scoop of houmous and a drizzle of tahini pomegranate hot sauce, top with a second squash slice, and finish with tahini sauce. Repeat with the remaining squash slices and serve immediately.

TAHINI CHICKEN CURRY

The original recipe for this curry came to me via a lifelong friend of a lifelong friend. You know a dish is good when it makes its way from home to home to home.

    Still, I couldn't help but tinker. I melted tahini into the already creamy sauce, lending it an incredible velvetiness, and added crushed pineapple to balance out the heat – honouring the origins of this much-loved dish while making it my own. **MAKES 4–6 SERVINGS**

6 tablespoons mild curry powder

1 tablespoon ground coriander

1 teaspoon chopped green cardamom pods

1 tablespoon ground cumin

1 tablespoon freshly ground black pepper

1 tablespoon ground turmeric

Pinch of saffron (optional)

8–12 skin-on chicken thighs (bone-in or boneless), rinsed and patted dry

120ml olive oil

1 shallot, diced

1 whole head garlic, peeled and sliced

4cm piece fresh ginger, peeled and sliced

1 long hot or other mild chilli, chopped (optional)

230g carrots cut into small cubes

450g fresh or frozen baby peas

25g chopped fresh coriander

240ml All-Purpose Tahini Sauce (page 209)

240ml unsweetened coconut milk

75g unsweetened crushed pineapple (tinned or fresh)

Sea salt

120ml cup fresh lemon juice

15g chopped fresh flat-leaf parsley

Cooked rice, for serving (optional)

In a small bowl, whisk together the curry powder, coriander, cardamom, cumin, black pepper, turmeric and saffron. Rub half of the spice mixture evenly over the chicken thighs, pressing gently so it adheres.

Heat 60ml of the oil in a wide, deep, heavy-based saucepan over a medium heat. Working in batches if needed, sear the chicken on both sides until golden, about 4 minutes per side. Set aside on a plate.

Using a slotted spoon, discard any bits of chicken or burned spices that remain in the pan. Heat the remaining 60ml oil in the same pan and add the shallot, garlic, ginger and chilli, if using, and cook until lightly browned, 3–5 minutes. Add the remaining half of the spice mixture and cook until fragrant, about 1 minute.

Add the carrots and peas, cover, and cook for about 5 minutes, then add the coriander, chicken and 1.4 litres of water.

Cover and cook for 30–40 minutes, adding more water if the pan becomes too dry, until the chicken is cooked through, but still moist. Add the tahini sauce, coconut milk and pineapple and cook for an additional 5 minutes. Season with salt and serve drizzled with the lemon juice and garnished with the parsley. Serve with rice, if desired.

NOTE: After searing the chicken, instead of finishing it on the hob, you can cook it in a 180°C/gas mark 4 oven in a covered heatproof baking dish for 30–40 minutes.

FIVE ONION CHICKEN

I caramelise onions in bulk to use as a base for countless dishes at the restaurant. I love how they transform, sweetening and softening, browning and mellowing, revealing an entirely different character depending on the length of time you cook them. I go for the palest gold to use in kibbeh stuffing, for instance, but commit to a burnished, frizzled brown for lentil pilafs, which really benefit from the profound savour and crunch.

One day, standing over a pan of these aromatic alliums, I thought that it was high time that onions had a chance to be the star of the show. So I cooked down five different varieties with a hint of curry powder and let the chicken take the supporting role. **MAKES 8 SERVINGS**

2 tablespoons sumac

1 tablespoon sweet chilli flakes or paprika

1 heaped tablespoon lemon pepper

1 tablespoon ground turmeric

1 tablespoon ground allspice

½ teaspoon freshly grated nutmeg

½ teaspoon ground cardamom

1½ teaspoons freshly ground black pepper

½ teaspoon ground cinnamon

15g chopped fresh coriander

1 teaspoon green curry powder, or 1 tablespoon green curry paste

2 chickens, cut into 8 pieces each (you can ask your butcher to do this)

120g olive oil

450g baby onions, peeled

10 shallots, thinly sliced

2 red onions, thinly sliced

1 large or 2 small white onions, sliced

4 leeks, white parts only, thinly sliced

2 poblano chillies, halved, deseeded and thinly sliced

6 medium waxy potatoes, peeled and cut into thin matchsticks

Sea salt

Juice of 2 lemons

Arabic bread (such as pitta or Flatbread, page 33), or Rice and Vermicelli Pilaf (page 140) and pickles, for serving

In a small bowl, whisk together the sumac, chilli flakes, lemon pepper, turmeric, allspice, nutmeg, cardamom, black pepper, cinnamon, coriander and green curry powder. Rub half of the spice mixture evenly over the chicken pieces, pressing gently so it adheres.

Heat the oil in a large, deep frying pan or saucepan over a medium heat. Working in batches if necessary, sear the chicken pieces on both sides until golden, about 4 minutes each side. Remove to a plate. Add the various onions, shallots and leeks, along with the chillis and potatoes to the frying pan. Cover and cook until softened and golden brown, 10–12 minutes. Turn the heat off and add the remaining half of the spice mixture.

Preheat the oven to 230°C/gas 8.

Place the chicken pieces in a large baking dish (use two dishes if necessary) and cover the chicken with the onion mixture. Sprinkle with salt. Pour 1 litre of water into the corners of the baking dish, cover with aluminium foil, and bake for 30 minutes. Reduce the oven temperature to 180°C/gas mark 4 and bake for another 10 minutes. Reduce the oven temperature to 150°C/gas mark 2, remove the foil, sprinkle with the lemon juice and roast for another 10 minutes, or until the chicken and onions are golden and crispy. Serve with Arabic bread and pickles or rice alongside.

HARISSA BAKED CHICKEN

Heat can register on the palate in a myriad of ways: a jalapeño lands differently than wasabi, and the same goes for black pepper and harissa. The latter is my favourite for imparting both flavour and fire, just assertive enough to jolt a dish while contributing intriguing, aromatic depth. **MAKES 4–8 SERVINGS**

2 chickens, halved or quartered (you can ask your butcher to do this)

2 tablespoons Tanoreen Spice Mix
  or
  1 tablespoon ground allspice
  1 teaspoon freshly grated nutmeg
  1 tablespoon ground cumin
  1 tablespoon freshly ground black pepper
  1 tablespoon ground ginger

120ml vegetable oil

8 waxy potatoes, sliced into 1.25cm-thick rounds

240ml olive oil

240ml Harissa (page 212, or shop-bought)

120ml fresh lemon juice

135g chopped shallots

2 tablespoons chopped garlic

2 poblano chillies, finely chopped

2 tablespoons crushed dried Persian limes (*limu omani*; optional, see sidebar)

4 tablespoons Coriander-Basil Pesto (page 216), or 8g chopped fresh basil and 8g chopped fresh coriander

1 litre chicken stock or water

Sea salt

Preheat the oven to 230°C/gas mark 8.

Place the chicken pieces in a large bowl. Rub 1 tablespoon of the Tanoreen Spices evenly over the chicken pieces, pressing gently so they adhere.

Heat the vegetable oil in a large, deep frying pan over a medium-high heat. Working in batches if necessary, sear the chicken pieces on both sides until golden, about 4 minutes each side.

In a large bowl, toss the potatoes with 120ml of the olive oil, then place them in a large baking dish. Roast until just golden, 20–25 minutes. Remove from the oven and place the seared chicken in a single layer on top of the potatoes. Return the dish to the oven and reduce the oven temperature to 180°C/gas mark 4.

In a small bowl, whisk together the remaining 120ml olive oil, the harissa, lemon juice, shallots, garlic, chillies, crushed dried limes, if using, the remaining 1 tablespoon Tanoreen Spices and the pesto. Brush evenly over the chicken.

Pour the chicken stock into the four corners of the baking dish, being careful not to let it splash on top of the chicken. Season everything with salt. Cover the dish with aluminium foil, place in the oven, and roast for 60–75 minutes, until the juices run clear when a knife is inserted between the leg and breast or a meat thermometer registers 74°C. Remove the foil and roast for 5 minutes more, or until golden all over and crispy, being careful not to let the harissa burn.

BAKED CHICKEN KIBBEH

You know you love to eat – and have friends and family who are food lovers too – when you throw a dinner party and instead of debating politics, you discuss food. This is how my chicken kibbeh recipe came about one winter night a few years ago.

On Monday evenings (my night off) when my son, Tarek, is in from Los Angeles, he enjoys cooking dinner so we can spend some quality time together. Dinner is always accompanied by lively conversation with lots of laughter. One evening we were all sitting around the kitchen island with an overflowing cheese board and my husband's famous endless wine pours. Tarek was preparing beef bourguignon when someone asked him if it could be made with chicken instead. Of course – it's coq au vin, the wine-braised chicken cousin of beef bourguignon. That got me thinking about other potential protein swaps and kibbeh, a dish that's traditionally off limits to non-red-meat eaters. I had made fish and vegan kibbehs in the past, but at that moment it occurred to me that chicken would be the closest substitute.

Chicken kibbeh has the benefit of being leaner and lower in cholesterol and saturated fat than the lamb version, yet it's every bit as flavourful and a worthy centrepiece for any Monday (or Friday) night dinner party. Not that you need to save it for special occasions – even if you're a family of four, three, two or just one. To be honest, any of my kibbeh recipes are actually better once frozen and reheated: just wrap any leftover squares in plastic to store them, then unwrap, and pop in the oven whenever you're ready to eat. **MAKES 12 SERVINGS**

STUFFING

120ml olive oil

3 onions, finely diced

2 shallots, finely diced

2 tablespoons Tanoreen Kibbeh Spice Mix
    or
    1 tablespoon dried marjoram
    1 tablespoon freshly ground black pepper
    1 tablespoon ground allspice
    Pinch of freshly grated nutmeg
    Pinch of ground cardamom
    ¼ teaspoon ground cinnamon

1.35kg boneless, skinless chicken thighs or breast, cut into 1.25cm cubes

1–2 tablespoons Hot Pepper Paste (page 212)

80g flaked almonds, toasted

65g pine nuts or 50g walnuts, toasted

Sea salt

OUTER LAYER

450g fine bulgar wheat, soaked in cold water to cover for 30 minutes

1 shallot, puréed in a food processor until almost liquid

900g boneless, skinless chicken breasts, chopped, then puréed into a paste in a food processor

2 tablespoons Tanoreen Kibbeh Spice Mix
    or
    1 tablespoon dried marjoram
    1 tablespoon freshly ground black pepper
    1 tablespoon ground allspice
    Pinch of freshly grated nutmeg
    Pinch of ground cardamom
    ¼ teaspoon ground cinnamon
    1 tablespoon ground cumin

Sea salt

120ml olive oil, for greasing

Make the stuffing: Heat the oil in a large frying pan over a medium heat. Add the onions and shallots and cook until very lightly browned, about 3 minutes. Add the kibbeh spice mix and stir to combine. Add the cubed chicken and hot pepper paste and cook until the chicken is cooked through, 15–20 minutes. Add the almonds and pine nuts and season with salt. Pour the stuffing into a colander placed over a bowl so the oil and juices drip into the bowl. Set the drained stuffing and bowl of drippings aside to cool.

Make the outer layer: In a large bowl, combine the soaked bulgar, puréed shallot, puréed chicken, and kibbeh spice mix. Season with salt. Dip your hands in a bowl of ice water to keep them moist, and mix with your hands until the ingredients are incorporated into a workable dough that holds its shape when pressed. Divide into two equal pieces.

Make the kibbeh: Preheat the oven to 200°C/ gas mark 6. Grease a 23 x 33cm baking pan with 4 tablespoons of the remaining oil.

Roll half of the kibbeh shell into a ball. Place the ball in the middle of the pan and spread it with your hands (dipping them into the ice water as needed) until it evenly covers the bottom of the pan and extends partially up the sides. Spread the stuffing in an even layer on top of the kibbeh shell.

Pinch off pieces of the remaining kibbeh shell dough and roll them into balls. Pat the balls so they are about 1.25cm thick (still keeping your hands moist) and evenly distribute them on top of the stuffing. Use your wet fingers to close the gaps between the dough so there is an even, flat layer of kibbeh shell on top of the stuffing.

Brush the kibbeh with the remaining 4 tablespoons oil and pour the reserved stuffing drippings over the top. Score the kibbeh into triangles, rectangles, or squares, making sure to cut only through the top layer of shell.

Bake the kibbeh for 15 minutes, then reduce the heat to 150°C/gas mark 2 and bake for an additional 25 minutes, or until golden brown. Cut along the scored lines and serve.

NOTE: As tasty as the stuffing is, you can use the shell to make kibbeh bowls or kibbeh cups for parties (page 60) and fill them with anything you wish!

CHICKEN & AUBERGINE ROLLATINI

Living and working in New York all these years — especially in Brooklyn, with its dynamic Italian-American population — I've learned the difference between an average slice of pizza and a life-changing one. The same is true of staples like chicken and aubergine rollatini, which are found across the menus of neighborhood Italian restaurants.

   In reimagining this popular dish, my goal was to add elements of freshness without sacrificing the sense of rustic comfort. So I tossed za'atar into the coating, tucked spinach, basil, and three kinds of cheese into the stuffing and used fresh tomatoes for the sauce. You're free to use a good jarred tomato sauce here, but the fresh sauce gives it the best texture. **MAKES 6 SERVINGS**

CHICKEN, AUBERGINE, AND COATING

85g panko breadcrumbs

40g shredded Parmesan cheese

15g finely chopped fresh parsley
(or 1 tablespoon dried parsley)

1 heaped tablespoon lemon pepper
(or black pepper mixed with lemon zest)

1 tablespoon dried basil

1 tablespoon dried oregano or za'atar

¼ teaspoon ground ginger

½ teaspoon garlic powder

1 teaspoon paprika

130g plain flour (or use gluten-free flour
or cornmeal)

4 large egg whites, beaten

6 boneless, skinless chicken breasts, butterflied
and thinly pounded (you can ask your
butcher to do this for you)

2 large Italian aubergines, cut lengthways into
3 even-size slices each

Vegetable oil, for frying

STUFFING

240ml Coriander-Basil Pesto (page 216) or
shop-bought pesto

115g grated kashkaval cheese (see page 50)

115g grated halloumi cheese

115g grated soft Mexican cheese such as queso
blanco (or Arabic cheese or mozzarella)

1 large bunch fresh basil

450g fresh spinach

24 oil-packed sun-dried tomatoes

12 slices fresh tomato

SAUCE

4 tablespoons olive oil, plus more for drizzling

1 tablespoon crushed garlic

680g chopped tomatoes

Sea salt

Freshly ground black pepper

Rice and Vermicelli Pilaf (see page 140)

(CONTINUED)

Coat and fry the chicken and aubergine: In a shallow dish, toss the panko with the Parmesan, parsley, lemon pepper, basil, oregano, ginger, garlic powder and paprika. Put the flour and beaten egg whites into two separate shallow dishes. Dredge the chicken cutlets in the flour, then the egg, then the breadcrumbs and set aside. Repeat with the aubergine slices.

Pour vegetable oil into a large frying pan to a depth of about 1.25cm. Heat until hot but not smoking. Fry the chicken cutlets and aubergine slices, working in batches if necessary, turning until they're just golden on all sides, pliable but not soft or cooked all the way. Place on kitchen paper to drain.

Stuff the chicken and aubergine: Spread about 1 teaspoon pesto over each of the chicken cutlets and aubergine slices, being careful not to break up the coating. Stack a scant teaspoon or so of each of the cheeses, followed by a few basil leaves, a few spinach leaves, a couple of sun-dried tomatoes, and a slice of fresh tomato on one side of each of the chicken cutlets and aubergine slices. Roll tightly jelly-roll style and place seam-side down on a baking tray.

Preheat the oven to 230°C/gas mark 8.

Make the sauce: Heat the olive oil in a medium saucepan over a medium heat. Add the garlic and cook until lightly browned, about 3 minutes. Season with salt and black pepper. Add the tomatoes and cook until they fall apart, about 15 minutes. Add any cheeses and pesto you have left from the stuffing and cook until the cheese melts and the sauce turns pink, about 5 minutes. Set aside.

Drizzle a large baking dish with olive oil and place the chicken rolls on it seam-side down. Bake for 5 minutes, flip the rolls over, and bake for an additional 5 minutes. Reduce the oven temperature to 200°C/gas mark 6. Drizzle half of the sauce over the chicken, cover the dish with aluminium foil, then return to the oven and bake for 20 minutes. Remove the foil and carefully nestle the aubergine rolls between the chicken rolls. Drizzle with the remaining sauce, replace the foil, and bake for another 10 minutes.

RICE & VERMICELLI PILAF

MAKES 8–10 SERVINGS

150ml olive oil

55g butter or ghee

450g vermicelli, broken into small pieces if the noodles are long

750g Egyptian, Chinese or other short-grain rice

2.1 litres boiling water

Sea salt

In a medium saucepan, heat the oil and butter over a medium heat. Add the vermicelli and cook, stirring frequently, until golden brown, about 5 minutes. Add the rice and cook until opaque, 3–5 minutes. Pour in the boiling water and season with salt. Reduce the heat to low, cover and cook until the rice is fluffy, stirring once halfway through, about 12 minutes. Turn off the heat, stir once more and let stand for 5 minutes before serving.

BAHRAINI CHICKEN WITH RICE

MACHBOUS

Machbous is very popular in the Gulf regions of the Middle East. I tried to replicate it using ingredients readily to hand and came up with this beautiful variation. **MAKES 6–8 SERVINGS**

7.5cm piece fresh turmeric, peeled and finely grated, or 2 tablespoons ground turmeric

1½ teaspoons saffron

1 tablespoon freshly ground black pepper

1 teaspoon ground cardamom

½ teaspoon freshly grated nutmeg

1 tablespoon ground cumin

1 tablespoon ground coriander

1 teaspoon chilli flakes

2 chickens, quartered (you can ask your butcher to do this)

240ml olive oil

5 shallots, diced

1 onion, diced

1 poblano chilli, diced

2 tablespoons diced garlic

1kg fresh or frozen and thawed artichoke hearts, thinly sliced

2 carrots, diced

2 potatoes, peeled and diced

1 bunch celery, diced

155g fresh or frozen peas

5cm piece fresh ginger, peeled and finely grated, or 1½ tablespoons ground ginger

Sea salt

3 bay leaves

240ml tamarind paste concentrate

7 dried Persian limes (*limu omani*), pricked a few times with a knife

25g fresh coriander

350g basmati rice

In a small bowl, combine the turmeric, saffron, black pepper, cardamom, nutmeg, cumin, coriander and chilli flakes. Place the chicken in a large bowl and rub with half of the spice mixture, making sure it's well coated on all sides. Marinate for 30–60 minutes.

Heat 120ml of the oil in a large heavy-based pan over a high heat until hot but not smoking. Sear the chicken for about 5 minutes on each side, then remove to a plate. Reduce the heat to medium, add the shallots and onions, and cook for 5–6 minutes, until translucent. Add the chilli and garlic and cook for 2 minutes. Add artichoke hearts, carrots, potatoes, celery and peas, cover and cook for 5 minutes, or until the vegetables start to soften. Add the remaining spice mixture and the ginger and season with salt. Remove one-third of the vegetable mixture from the pan to a bowl and set aside.

Return the chicken to the pan, add the bay leaves and 1.9 litres water and bring to a simmer over a medium heat. Cook for 20 minutes, skimming off any foam. Remove 950ml of liquid from the pan and set aside. Add the tamarind, five of the *limu*, and the coriander to the pan and simmer until the chicken is cooked through, about 40 minutes. Season with salt.

Heat the remaining oil in a deep frying pan over a medium heat. Add the rice and cook for 3–4 minutes, until well coated. Add the reserved vegetables, stock, and the two remaining *limu*. Bring to the boil, reduce the heat to a simmer, cover, and cook for 20 minutes or until rice is tender, stirring once after 5 minutes. Season with salt. Spoon onto a platter and top with the chicken and vegetables. Drizzle over some of the leftover liquid from the frying pan as a sauce.

TANOREEN SPICED POUSSINS

Growing up, we would often drive three long hours to Bethlehem to visit a restaurant called Farouj, which served only its single, namesake item – small grilled butterflied chicken. That, and fiery glasses of the anise-flavoured spirit called arak. Needless to say, a dish worthy of such a trip was one I felt compelled to re-create when I moved to the United States. I looked everywhere for tiny chicken, but with no luck.

Finally, I found my prize at a local Italian butcher. I excitedly took my birds home and threw them on the grill, but when we went to eat them, they were so tough they were almost inedible.

I went back to the butcher and he laughed – I hadn't purchased chickens at all, but Cornish hens (called poussin in some countries), which are younger, leaner, and contain more white meat than dark and thus are more prone to drying out. And so I came up with a compromise.

Since you can't simply throw a giant chicken on the grill, I stuck with the poussins, but I roasted them in the oven first so they would cook gently inside. Then I finished them quickly on the grill so the outside would develop that smoky flavour and gorgeous colour of authentic farouj. In the end, it was well worth all that time spent searching and experimenting, because nowadays the journey to Jerusalem takes me a whole lot longer than three hours. **MAKES 6 SERVINGS AS A MAIN DISH**

6 poussins, butterflied and flattened
  (you can ask your butcher to do this)

6 plum tomatoes, chopped

2 tablespoons chopped garlic

3 shallots, chopped

Leaves from 2 sprigs rosemary

1 fresh sage leaf

15g chopped fresh coriander

3 tablespoons Coriander-Basil Pesto (page 216) or
  shop-bought pesto

120ml olive oil

120ml fresh lemon juice

240ml white wine (optional)

1 tablespoon freshly ground black pepper

1½ teaspoons ground cumin

1 tablespoon Tanoreen Spice Mix
  or
  1 tablespoon ground allspice
  ½ teaspoon ground coriander
  ¼ teaspoon freshly grated nutmeg
  ½ teaspoon ground cardamom
  ½ teaspoon ground ginger

5 food-grade rosebuds (optional)

1 long hot or poblano chilli, chopped

1½ tablespoons sea salt

Vegetable oil, for brushing

Green salad, fattoush or grilled vegetables,
  for serving

(CONTINUED)

Place the poussins in a large bowl or baking dish.

Combine the remaining ingredients in a blender and blend until smooth. Pour half of the marinade over the poussins, using your hands to make sure it coats the birds completely, including under the skin. Cover and refrigerate for at least 2 hours or, ideally, overnight. Chill the remaining marinade in the refrigerator in a separate container.

Preheat the oven to 200°C/gas mark 6.

Remove the poussins from the marinade and wipe away any excess. Place in a roasting pan, cover with aluminium foil and roast for 35–40 minutes, until the birds are close to, but not completely cooked through.

Place the birds in a large bowl or platter and cover with the reserved marinade. At this point, you can finish cooking the hens or keep them in the refrigerator until you're ready to serve (they will keep for up to 3 days).

Brush a grill or griddle pan with vegetable oil. Grill the hens over a low to medium heat (the slower you can cook them, the better). Grill for 15 minutes, or until the juices run clear when you cut into the breast, or a meat thermometer inserted into the breast registers 74°C.

Serve with green salad, *fattoush*, or grilled vegetables (you can toss the grilled vegetables in some of the reserved marinade before cooking).

Oil as Good as Gold

Growing up in Nazareth I remember my family pressing our own olive oil every season, and today my relatives still continue that tradition. Olive oil holds a central and cherished role in our cuisine. There are many varieties of oils available on the market today, but I still stick to these two for the most part:

EXTRA VIRGIN OLIVE OIL: Darker and greener in colour, extra virgin olive oil can have a flavour ranging from slightly fruity to spicy depending on the region. Use this in salad dressings, sautés, fresh quick sauces or dips. It's also great just as a finishing drizzle. You don't want to deep-fry with extra virgin olive oil, though; it has a low burning point and will smoke easily.

VIRGIN OLIVE OIL: Use this more neutral oil when you don't want the prominent taste of the extra virgin variety interfering with the taste of the dish. This has a higher burning point than the extra virgin variety so you can easily fry with it.

BRAISED BEEF & MUSHROOMS
WITH ALMOND TEKLAI

The addition of fresh green za'atar to this rib-sticking stew is a revelation, as the dynamic herb really cuts through all of that deep, long-simmered richness. The toasty almond teklai on top adds a fantastic crunchy contrast (you could also toss the teklai with pasta). If enoki mushrooms aren't available use button, oyster or portobello mushrooms; each will lend its own texture and character. To make this dish gluten-free, use gluten-free breadcrumbs. **MAKES 8–10 SERVINGS**

STEW

1 teaspoon ground allspice

¼ teaspoon ground cinnamon

¼ teaspoon ground cardamom

2 teaspoons paprika, preferably smoked

2 tablespoons fresh green za'atar, or 1 tablespoon
    dried za'atar

1 tablespoon sea salt, or to taste

1 tablespoon freshly ground black pepper, or to taste

120ml olive oil

1.35–1.8kg beef, such as top round, fillet, or sirloin,
    cut into 4cm cubes

675g enoki mushrooms, trimmed and cleaned

3 onions, diced

4 shallots, diced

1 tablespoon honey

720ml white wine (or water, plus the juice of 1 lemon)

4 bay leaves

6 plum tomatoes, peeled and sliced lengthways

TEKLAI

6 tablespoons olive oil

1 tablespoon diced garlic

1 long hot, jalapeño, or poblano chilli, diced (optional)

25g unseasoned breadcrumbs (I prefer panko)

60g chopped almonds

15g chopped fresh flat-leaf parsley

Lemon slices, for serving

Make the stew: In a small bowl, whisk together the allspice, cinnamon, cardamom, paprika, za'atar, salt and pepper. Rub half of the spice mixture onto the meat, using your hands to make sure it's coated evenly.

Heat 4 tablespoons of the oil in a large saucepan over a medium heat. Working in batches if necessary, add the beef and sear until browned on all sides, about 2 minutes per side. Transfer the meat to a plate. Add the remaining oil to the pan, then add the mushrooms. Cook until the mushrooms just begin to colour but haven't started to release their liquid, about 3 minutes. Transfer the mushrooms to a plate. Add the onions and shallots to the pan and cook until translucent, about 4 minutes. Return the beef to the pan, add the honey, and stir to coat the beef. Add 720ml water, the wine, bay leaves, tomatoes and the remaining spice mixture. Stir to combine and bring to the boil. Reduce the heat to a simmer, cover and cook for 1½ hours. Add the reserved mushrooms and cook for 30 minutes more, or until the beef is fork-tender.

Make the teklai: Heat the oil in a small frying pan over a medium heat. Add the garlic and cook until fragrant but not coloured, for 1 minute. Add the chilli, if using, and cook until softened, about 3 minutes. Add the breadcrumbs and almonds and cook until toasty and browned, 2–3 minutes. Add the parsley and cook until barely wilted, about 30 seconds.

Spoon the stew into bowls and serve with the hot teklai on top and lemon slices alongside.

ALEPPO-STYLE KIBBEH STEW
WITH CARROTS

I love carrots . . . cooked. I find them so much sweeter and more vivid as they deepen in flavour and colour while they cook. One of my favourite methods to cook carrots is to steam them until just tender and toss them with hot olive oil, garlic, coriander, and, of course, a big squeeze of lemon. However, if you have a bit more time on your hands, you can transform the humble carrot into something truly spectacular.

My best friend of forty-five years, Yolanda, brought this kibbeh dish to my attention after she tried it at a Syrian friend's home one night. As she is practically my sister, she knew enough to report back on a carrot-centric dish in the Middle Eastern kitchen I was not familiar with.

Here big hunks of sweet carrot are cooked low and slow along with silky squares of beef in a cardamom-perfumed stock of tangy pomegranate juice, smoky poblano and tamarind. For the pièce de résistance, crispy, bite-size kibbeh balls are dropped on top at the last minute, making this the perfect centrepiece for a Sunday supper, started in the morning so it fills the house with gorgeous, toasty aromas throughout the day. **MAKES 8–10 SERVINGS**

STEW

240ml olive oil

5 cardamom pods, crushed

5 or 6 bay leaves

2 tablespoons Tanoreen Spice Mix
    or
    1 tablespoon ground allspice
    ½ teaspoon ground cinnamon
    Pinch of freshly grated nutmeg

1.35kg boneless stewing beef, cut into 5cm cubes

2 shallots, diced

25g chopped fresh coriander

120g chopped poblano chillies or green peppers

2 tablespoons chopped garlic

3 extra-large or 6 large carrots, cut into 7.5cm chunks

240ml unsweetened pomegranate juice

480ml tomato juice

480ml tamarind paste concentrate

Sea salt

1 batch Lamb Kibbie dough (page 60)

Vegetable oil, for frying

Make the stew: Heat 120ml of the olive oil in a large saucepan set over a medium heat. Add the cardamom, bay leaves and Tanoreen spices and cook until aromatic, about 1 minute. Add the beef, mix to distribute the spices and cook for about 5 minutes, stirring occasionally, until the meat browns on all sides. Add 1.9 litres water, increase the heat to high and bring to the boil. Cover the pan, reduce the heat to low, and cook for 1–1 ½ hours, until the meat is fork-tender.

While the meat is cooking, heat the remaining 120ml olive oil in a separate large saucepan over a medium heat. Add the shallots, coriander, chillies and garlic and cook until the vegetables are softened, about 4 minutes. Add the carrots, cover, reduce the heat to low and cook until the carrots are crisp-tender, about 10 minutes. Add the pomegranate juice,

(CONTINUED)

tomato juice, tamarind paste, and 960ml cooking liquid from the pan of beef. (Strain the rest of the liquid from the pot of beef and use as stock in another recipe.) Increase the heat to high and bring to the boil. Add the braised beef, cover the pan, reduce the heat to medium and cook until the carrots are tender, 10–15 minutes. Season with salt.

Roll the lamb kibbeh dough into 1.25cm balls. Pour enough vegetable oil into a frying pan to reach a depth of 2.5cm. Heat until hot, but not smoking. Fry the kibbeh in batches until golden brown and crisp on all sides, about 10 minutes, or 5 minutes a deep-fat fryer. Ladle the beef stew into bowls and top each with 3–5 pieces of kibbeh.

NOTE: If you'd rather skip the kibbeh, the stew is fantastic served over buttered noodles, orzo or rice.

Stuff It All!

Throughout the Levant, you will find mashi vegetables—meaning they are cored, stuffed, and stewed. Every house, in every town and city, cooks a variation on this dish. The type of vegetable used imparts its flavor both to its stuffing and the surrounding sauce (typically tomato), creating a perfect food marriage.

The most traditional vegetables for mashi are squash, eggplant, and bell peppers; I like to try other veggies such as turnips (page 112) and tomatoes (page 40). Each vessel is stuffed to the brim, most often with spiced ground lamb and rice or a vegan tabouleh-like mixture, then simmered slow and steady.

My mother taught me to make sure to fit mashi snuggly together in the pot standing upright (not floating around) to ensure the stuffing would stay inside each vegetable. But on the odd occasion when she came up short with extra space left in the pot, she would grab a potato, core and stuff it, and stick it in as a placeholder. Problem solved.

Here's the irony: Although it was the redheaded stepchild in this scenario, guess what everyone at the table fought over when supper was served? The potato. So, here I wanted to give it some time in the spotlight.

In my version, I switched out the thick tomato sauce for a lighter, brighter lemony tamarind sauce that contrasts with the tender potatoes and hearty lamb stuffing. This is meat and potatoes my way, and it's my husband's favorite dish to boot.

LAMB-STUFFED POTATOES
IN TAMARIND SAUCE

In the Middle Eastern kitchen, we stuff almost every vegetable you can think of, from squash and aubergine to peppers, turnips and even carrots. Since they're natural vessels, potatoes get the *mashi* (stuffed) treatment too. Stuffed potatoes are traditionally deep-fried to create a tempting crust, but it's not too much of a sacrifice to bake them instead. And instead of simmering them in a tomato sauce stew, a bath of chicken stock and tamarind paste lightens them up. Think of this as a slimmed-down version of meat and potatoes! **MAKES 8 STUFFED POTATOES**

Juice of 2 lemons, plus more for spritzing

8 large baking potatoes, peeled

6 tablespoons olive oil, plus more for roasting

135g chopped shallots

6 cloves garlic, chopped

1½ tablespoons Tanoreen Spice Mix plus
    1½ teaspoons freshly ground black pepper
    or
    1 tablespoon ground allspice
    ½ teaspoon ground cumin
    ½ teaspoon ground cinnamon
    ½ teaspoon ground cardamom
    1½ teaspoons freshly ground black pepper
    Pinch of freshly grated nutmeg

25g chopped fresh coriander

900g minced meat (preferably a tender cut such as leg of lamb or beef sirloin)

80g flaked almonds, toasted

65g pine nuts, toasted (optional)

1 tablespoon sea salt, or to taste

480ml chicken stock or water

420ml tamarind paste concentrate

1 long hot or jalapeño chilli, thinly sliced (optional)

Carefully insert an apple corer in the long end of each potato, pushing it all the way through in order to remove the flesh from the centres. Use a teaspoon to create a bigger cavity, scraping away a bit more of the interior flesh and leaving about 1cm on each side. Place the potato flesh in a baking dish large enough to eventually fit the 8 potato shells and spritz with lemon juice so it doesn't discolour.

Heat the oil in a large frying pan over a medium heat. Add the shallots, garlic, Tanoreen spices and coriander and cook until softened and fragrant, about 4 minutes. Add the meat and cook until lightly browned, about 5 minutes. Add the almonds, pine nuts, if using, and salt and stir to combine. Remove from the heat and set aside to cool.

Stuff the potato shells with the meat mixture and brush them with oil. Lay the potato shells flat over the reserved potato flesh in the baking dish and sprinkle with salt.

In a medium bowl, whisk together the water, tamarind paste, lemon juice, chillies, if using, and a sprinkle of salt if desired. Pour the mixture into the four corners of the baking dish. Cover the dish with aluminium foil and bake for 30–40 minutes, until the potatoes are tender, checking after 10–15 minutes to see if the pan is looking dry. If so, add another cup of water. Serve covered with pan sauce.

SWEET & SOUR BEEF ROLLS

From Italian braciole to German rouladen and Japanese negimaki, beef roll-ups are common to many cultures. For my version, I season the beef with my blend of signature aromatic spices, fill my pinwheels with halloumi cheese and spring onions and instead of the sticky soy sauce negimaki is known for, I reduce red wine and pomegranate juice for a multidimensional sweetness and glaze-like consistency. The sky is the limit when it comes to stuffing — try turnips instead of carrots, thyme instead of sage and Emmental or Jarlsberg instead of halloumi. **MAKES 4 SERVINGS AS A MAIN COURSE OR 8 SERVINGS AS A MEZZE**

1 tablespoon ground coriander

1 tablespoon ground cumin

1 tablespoon ground allspice

½ teaspoon freshly grated nutmeg

½ teaspoon ground cardamom

1 tablespoon freshly ground black pepper

8 slices beef (such as topside, fillet or sirloin), approximately 0.5cm thick, 12.5cm wide, and 25cm long

2 carrots, cut into 4 strips each (about 12.5cm long)

8 spring onions, trimmed

1 bulb fennel, top trimmed off, cored, and cut into 8 strips

225g (1 block) halloumi cheese, cut into 8 slices

16 fresh sage leaves

1 poblano or long hot chilli, cut into 8 strips (optional)

120ml vegetable oil

4 shallots, diced

8 cloves garlic, diced

25g chopped fresh coriander

480ml dry red wine, or 120ml red wine vinegar

480ml unsweetened pomegranate juice, plus more if needed

480ml tomato juice, preferably fresh, plus more if needed

480ml beef or vegetable stock, plus more if needed

Sea salt

In a small bowl, whisk together the spices. Rub half of the spice mixture evenly over the beef slices, pressing gently so it adheres.

Starting at one of the short sides of a slice of beef, group together 1 carrot slice, 1 spring onion (folded in half), 1 fennel strip, 1 halloumi strip, 2 sage leaves and 1 chilli slice, if using. Roll tightly Swiss-roll style and use a toothpick to secure the seam end, if needed. Repeat with the remaining ingredients.

Heat the oil in a large, wide, deep saucepan over a medium heat. Working in batches if needed, add the beef rolls and sear until deeply browned on all sides, about 4 minutes per side. Remove the beef to a plate. Add the shallots to the oil and cook until golden, 3–5 minutes. Add the garlic and cook until fragrant, about 2 minutes. Add the coriander and cook until wilted. Add the remaining half of the spice mixture and cook for a few seconds, or until the spices release their fragrance. Add the wine and pomegranate and tomato juice. Bring to the boil, add the stock, and season with salt.

Set the beef rolls in the pan and bring back to the boil. Reduce the heat to low, cover, and cook for 1½–2 hours, until the meat is fork-tender, checking every 10 minutes or so to make sure the rolls are half submerged. If necessary, add a bit more juice or stock.

Uncover the pan and cook until the beef caramelises and the sauce thickens. Season with salt. Cut into bite-size slices for appetisers, or serve whole as a main dish, alongside rice or mashed potatoes.

LIKE WATER FOR POMEGRANATES

From water there was wine. And equally miraculous is the alchemy-like conversion of pomegranate juice to thick, fruity molasses. You'll see that my analogy has merit, as both are connected to the Palestinian village of Kafr Cana in the Lower Galilee, where according to Christian tradition, Jesus famously transformed water to wine when he attended a poor couple's wedding.

The tiny Kafr Cana is about a mile from Nazareth. And because the surrounding villages were also small (at least while I was growing up), families bussed their children into the Nazareth schools. One of my friends was from this neighbouring town, and when our school bus drove through the winding village road to her house, I couldn't help but admire the jewel-studded pomegranate trees that were growing everywhere. The town was famous for farming and harvesting these fruits to make drinks, desserts and of course, pomegranate molasses, to sell at local markets.

We children would sit under the hovering branches, pick fruit, and dig into them with abandon, staining our clothes on almost every occasion. My mother was less than pleased about the mess, but her irritation was quickly forgotten when I would return home with bags full of the fruit.

My friend's parents taught me which of these seed-filled wonders were best to pick, and for what purpose. The smaller, baseball-size ones, still tart, were left to ripen, while the grapefruit-size specimens were perfect for desserts and juice. Then there were the sharabi, or medium-size variety, which were uniformly sweet and sour. These were used to make molasses.

Back then, carob, grape or pomegranate molasses (common in most pantries) were almost exclusively used for drinks or dessert, almost never for savoury cooking. As it happened, I discovered the manifold properties of this special syrup while eating at the homes of my Syrian, Lebanese and Iraqi friends — in Brooklyn. We would take turns hosting dinners at each other's homes, usually with families in tow. It was at these convivial meals that pomegranate, in all its forms, became one of my holy grail ingredients in one fell swoop. That's where my love affair with the magical sweet and sour fruit reignited, and it continues to this day, as I drizzle concentrated, complex molasses onto everything from roasts and stews to salad dressings, sauces and marinades. Although the journey from under the pomegranate trees of Kafr Cana to my New York City kitchen was a long one, it was well worth every seed.

TO JUICE A POMEGRANATE: Either cut the pomegranate in half on its equator, or cut a 1.25cm sliver off one end, then cut four slits from top to bottom so that the pomegranate splits apart in a star formation. Place the fruit in one hand, skin-side up, over a sieve set over a large bowl. Using the flat side of a large knife, a heavy wooden spoon, or a pestle from a pestle and mortar set, tap on the skin all over, going round and round several times. This loosens the seeds so they will fall into the sieve below. After the seeds are all in the strainer, pick out any white membranes with your fingers and discard. Squeeze the seeds in your hands to release the juice.

BEEF STEW
WITH QUINCE

A kind of alchemy happens when you cook quince. It goes from dry and astringent to lusciously sweet and jammy and because of its high pectin content, it thickens this burgundy-hued stew beautifully.

Safarjal is Arabic for quince, which lends itself to the name of this dish, *safarjaliyyeh*. It is popular in Syria and can be served on its own or with Rice and Vermicelli Pilaf (page 140). There is a fancier version called *saffarjaliyya*, which features small lamb kibbeh balls and even more sumac added to the stew. If you're adventurous and want to give it a try, you'll find the recipe for making lamb kibbeh on page 60.

MAKES 6–8 SERVINGS

180ml olive oil

1 tablespoon ground allspice

1 tablespoon freshly ground black pepper

½ teaspoon freshly grated nutmeg

1 teaspoon ground cumin

1 tablespoon ground coriander

6 shallots, diced

2 tablespoons chopped garlic (about 6 cloves)

1 long hot or poblano chilli, finely diced

15g chopped fresh coriander

675g fillet steak (you can also use topside or sirloin), cut into 2.5cm cubes

2 tablespoons tomato purée

720ml tomato juice

720ml unsweetened pomegranate juice, or 120ml pomegranate molasses

Sea salt

4–6 quince, peeled, cored, and sliced vertically into 8 wedges (squeeze lemon juice on top to keep from discolouring)

2 tablespoons sumac

In a small bowl, whisk together the allspice, black pepper, nutmeg, cumin and coriander.

Heat 120ml of the oil in a large saucepan over a medium heat. Add the shallots and cook for 3 minutes, until softened. Add the garlic and chilli and cook until the shallots start to brown, about 5 minutes. Add the coriander and cook for 1 minute. Add half of the spice mixture to the pan and stir until the spices start to release their aroma, about 1 minute.

Add the beef and cook until it starts to sear and darken in colour all over, 5–7 minutes. Add the tomato purée and cook for 1 minute. Add the tomato juice, pomegranate juice and 480ml water and bring to the boil. Reduce the heat and simmer uncovered for 30 minutes (if using fillet steak) to 1 hour (if using a tougher cut), until the meat is tender. Season with salt.

Heat the remaining 60ml oil in a medium frying pan over a medium heat. Add the remaining spice mixture and stir to combine. Add the quince and cook until it starts to colour. Turn off the heat and add the cooked quince mixture to the stew. Add the sumac and bring to the boil. Reduce the heat to low and simmer, uncovered, for 20 minutes. Remove the stew and place in a large bowl to serve.

BRAISED OXTAIL
WITH OLIVES

In the early 1980s, my husband owned a supermarket in a neighbourhood of Brooklyn. One of his employees, Jimmy, an Italian-American in his late seventies, used to cook us authentic Italian meals at least once a week. One of his specialities was oxtail cacciatore, and Jimmy familiarised me with this inexpensive cut that can handle long cooking. His technique of stewing the oxtail in a ragout of vegetables reminded me of how in the Galilee and beyond a similar cut of meat would be tucked under stuffed grape leaves to prevent the leaves from burning. This oxtail is beyond fork-tender and the vegetables that accompany it melt into a virtual sauce that begs to be soaked up by rice pilaf or good crusty bread. I think Jimmy would have been pleased. **MAKES 8–10 SERVINGS**

2 whole oxtails, cut into 4cm pieces
    (ask your butcher to do this)

120g stoned green olives

350g diced onions

135g diced shallots

1 tablespoon chopped garlic

240g diced carrots

250g diced waxy potatoes

330g diced tomatoes

25g chopped fresh coriander

120g chopped long hot or poblano chillies (optional)

Juice of 2 lemons

120ml olive oil

2 tablespoons Hot Pepper Paste (page 212; optional)

1 tablespoon freshly ground black pepper

1 tablespoon ground allspice

1 tablespoon ground coriander

1 tablespoon ground cumin

1 teaspoon ground cardamom

1 tablespoon ground turmeric

Pinch of freshly grated nutmeg

Sea salt

Rice pilaf or crusty bread, for serving

Preheat the oven to 230°C/gas mark 8.

Place the oxtails in a large bowl and add the olives, onions, shallots, garlic, carrots, potatoes, tomatoes, coriander and chillies, if using and mix with your hands to combine.

In a separate bowl, whisk together the lemon juice, oil, hot pepper paste, if using, black pepper, allspice, coriander, cumin, cardamom, turmeric and nutmeg and season with salt. Pour the mixture over the meat and vegetables. Using your hands, mix to evenly coat.

Transfer the meat and vegetables to a large roasting pan and pour 720ml water into the sides of the pan. Cover with aluminium foil and bake for 1 hour. Reduce the oven temperature to 150°C/gas mark 2 and bake for another 1½ hours, or until the meat is so tender it practically melts when you poke it with a fork. Serve over rice pilaf or with crusty bread.

HOLIDAY ROASTED LEG OF LAMB

In the late 1980s my brother Marwan moved to Paris, and when Christmas rolled around, he flew my family over to experience the city of lights during this festive time. I was happily tasked with preparing the big dinner. Our tradition calls for leg of lamb, so Marwan and the kids went out to buy the meat, proudly carrying back not one but three whole legs! I decided on a red-wine marinade, inspired by the French surroundings.

As we tucked in at the table, my brother, husband and son played a prank: Each picked up a whole leg of lamb and took a bite right off the bone. The moment is immortalized in a photo that we still laugh about today, and I make this recipe every year around the holidays, always remembering that magical family trip. **MAKES 10–12 SERVINGS**

1 (2.3–3.2kg) bone-in leg of lamb

480ml red wine (or beef stock)

135g finely diced shallot

1 tablespoon finely diced garlic

3 dried bay leaves, crumbled

3 tablespoons Tanoreen Spice Mix
    or
    3 tablespoons ground allspice
    1½ teaspoons ground coriander
    1 teaspoon freshly grated nutmeg
    1 teaspoon ground cardamom
    1 teaspoon ground ginger

45g butter or ghee, at room temperature

900g yellow or red new potatoes

450g baby carrots

450g baby onions, peeled

Sea salt

Place the lamb in a large baking dish and pour the wine or stock over. In a small bowl, mix together the shallot, garlic, bay leaves and spices and rub the mixture evenly all over the lamb, pressing so it adheres. Cover the lamb with clingfilm and let marinate in the refrigerator for at least three hours or overnight.

Preheat the oven to 230°C/gas mark 8.

Set the lamb in a large roasting dish (you can discard the leftover marinade). Coat the lamb evenly with the butter and season with salt. Arrange the potatoes, carrots, and baby onions around the lamb. Cover the pan with parchment paper, followed by a tightly wrapped layer of aluminium foil. Roast the lamb for 30 minutes, then reduce the oven temperature to 150°C/gas mark 2. Roast for another 30 minutes, then turn the lamb, cover again, and roast for another hour. Uncover the lamb and roast for 5–10 minutes, until it's golden brown all over. Remove from the oven and let rest for 10–20 minutes.

To carve, place the lamb on its side on a chopping board. Starting on the outside, cut thin slices parallel to the bone until you reach the bone. Transfer the slices to a platter.

Turn the leg onto the cut side so that it sits level. Begin slicing the meat perpendicular to the bone. Once the knife hits the bone, continue slicing across the meat and above the bone until you reach the end of the leg.

To separate the meat slices from the bone, make a long horizontal slice along the top of it. Transfer the slices to the platter.

ONE LEG OF LAMB, ENDLESS OPTIONS

A whole roast of any kind can be intimidating to a home cook, but I want to reassure you that cooking larger cuts of meat is actually easier and can be more forgiving than using smaller cuts. All you need to consider is seasoning (use a liberal hand!) and timing (low and slow is generally best). The goal is to maintain a juicy succulent flavor all the way through.

Leg of lamb is one of the first dishes I learned to make for at-home dinner parties. It looks fancy enough for a holiday or formal gathering but in reality takes a minimum of effort. And the best part is that most of the preparation happens the night before, so all you need to do is put it in the oven the next day and let it perfume your home.

On the other hand, unless you're preparing for a big party, a whole bone-in lamb leg may not seem worth the effort (or expense). In that case, how about investing in a boneless leg. It can pay out dividends, as various cuts can turn into entirely different dinners. You don't need to be a brilliant butcher. With that big, pesky bone out of the way, you can easily divide the lamb as suggested below and freeze for future use.

KEBABS: Cut cubes for making shish kebabs (or finely dice for kofta kebabs) from the fattiest, most tender sirloin end of the leg, which will remain moist and juicy with quick grilling.

SHAWARMA: No, you don't need a special spit. As you'll see in my Sliders recipe (page 57), it's perfectly acceptable to chop up a tender section of meat (such as the thicker, sirloin end of the lamb leg). Then the meat can be liberally coated in spices, quickly seared and paired with pickles and pitas for irresistible sandwiches.

KIBBEH: You'll want to use the silkiest meat that's free of gristle and fat. That said, pure tenderloin is almost too lean, as once you finely chop it, it can get unappealingly mushy. So aim for the centre of the leg, which has the benefit of being connective tissue–free yet is still close enough to the muscles to pack an umami punch. The same goes if you'd like to mince lamb for Kibbeh Cups (page 60) or for the kibbie in Aleppo-Style Kibbeh Stew (page 146).

STUFFING: If you'd like to make your own minced lamb for stuffed dishes like Spicy Lamb Egg Rolls (page 47) or Lamb-Stuffed Potatoes (page 149), you'll generally want to go for the silky but toothsome center cut of the leg, or else you'll end up with paste.

STEW MEAT: Gather slow-cooking cubes from the narrow shank end, which is the brawniest, most muscular part of the leg. They're ideal for sumptuous braises enhanced with toasted spices, heady wine or fresh herbs. Feel free to swap lamb for beef in the Aleppo-Style Kibbie Stew (page 146), Beef Stew with Quince (page 154), or Beef & Mushroom Stew (page 145).

PAN-ROASTED SALMON
WITH SALSA KHADRA

My son is a pescatarian and loves his salmon: smoked, raw, seared, poached. So I created this easy, ready-in-minutes weeknight meal on one of his visits from California, famously home to virtuous eaters who are diligent about getting their daily dose of omega-3s.

It's a common misconception that Middle Eastern cooking doesn't make use of fresh herbs like dill, basil and coriander. This dish proves them wrong. While we're certainly known for rib-sticking soups and stews, we appreciate bright and light flavours as much as anyone. Even, dare I say it, health-conscious Californians. This salmon is wonderful accompanied by Artichoke & Tomato Sauté (page 83).

While salmon is a go-to source of omega-3 fatty acids, it has become common practice to remove the skin, which is where most of those fatty acids are found. Marinating and pan-searing enables the skin to absorb the flavours of the dish and helps it get wonderfully browned and crisp. **MAKES 6 SERVINGS**

6 skin-on salmon fillets

SALSA
15g fresh basil
15g fresh coriander
3 tablespoons fresh dill
8 cloves garlic, peeled
1 shallot
1 long hot or poblano chilli
1 tablespoon ground cumin
Juice of 2 lemons
4 stalks lemongrass, chopped
1 tablespoon sesame oil
3 tablespoons dark soy sauce

180ml olive oil, for cooking

Place the salmon fillets in a nonreactive pan. Combine the salsa ingredients in a food processor and pulse to combine. Pour half of the salsa over the salmon and let marinate for at least 1 hour.

Heat 60ml of the oil in a large frying pan over a medium heat. Add 2 salmon fillets to the pan skin-side down. Cook for 6–8 minutes, pressing gently on the back of the fillets a few times to prevent them from curling. Carefully flip the fillets and cook on the second side for 15 seconds. Repeat with the remaining fish and oil. Serve drizzled with spoonfuls of the remaining salsa and more on the side.

WALNUT-CRUSTED FISH FILLETS

My sister used to make a walnut-crusted chicken I adored. And I figured it would be just as good with fish, as the delicate flaky fillets are a beautiful contrast to the sturdy, savoury nuts. This recipe is ideal for a dinner party, as it's quite easy to make and versatile. You can substitute pistachios or almonds, or halve the recipe for a more intimate meal. It's especially elegant served with sautéed asparagus.

Marinating the fish adds that extra layer of flavour so it's not overwhelmed by the richness of the crust. **MAKES 8 SERVINGS**

MARINADE AND FISH

1 cup Coriander-Basil Pesto (page 216) or
    shop-bought pesto

Juice of 1 lemon

120ml olive oil

Sea salt and freshly ground black pepper

8 x 115g fillets of cod, hake
    or another firm white-fleshed fish

COATING

420g chopped walnuts

85g panko breadcrumbs

80g shredded Parmesan cheese

1 tablespoon lemon pepper (or black pepper
    sprinkled with lemon zest)

1 tablespoon paprika

1 tablespoon dried dill

390g plain flour (can use gluten-free or cornmeal)

4 large egg whites

Sea salt and freshly ground black pepper

Olive oil, for greasing

Rice and Vermicelli Pilaf (page 140) or a salad
    (such as Fennel, Pomegranate & Sage Salad,
    page 68), for serving

Marinate the fish: In a large, nonreactive bowl or baking dish, whisk together the pesto, lemon juice and oil. Season the fish with salt and pepper. Add the fish to the marinade and turn with your hands to evenly coat it. Place in the refrigerator to marinate for at least 30 minutes or up to 1 hour.

Preheat the oven to 180°C/gas mark4.

Coat the fish: In a shallow bowl, mix all the coating ingredients together. Place the flour and egg whites into separate shallow bowls and beat the egg whites with a pinch each of salt and pepper. Dip each fillet in the flour to lightly coat it on all sides, then dip in the egg white, followed by the coating mixture. Lightly tap the fillets on the side of the bowl to remove any excess coating.

Drizzle a large baking tray with oil and arrange the fillets on the pan in a single layer. Cover with aluminium foil and bake for 10 minutes, then remove the foil and cook for another 5 minutes, or until the fillets are golden and crispy. Serve with rice or salad alongside.

GO FISH

Because of our proximity to the Mediterranean, it's hard to compete with the Middle East's wealth of gorgeous fish. But while many of my food memories are tied to those pristine waters, I've been equally entranced by fish found closer to my new home, such as beautiful striped bass caught off the coast of Montauk, New York.

INSTEAD OF HAMOUR, TRY HADDOCK: Five years ago I visited the Persian Gulf area and was introduced there to a fish called hamour. It has little bones and a flavor that is not too fishy. It was by far one of the most delicious fish I've ever tasted; I knew I would use it frequently in my cooking. Hamour most directly refers to brown-spotted grouper, though it's become a catchall term for a variety of species in the Persian Gulf. Really, any type of lean, firm white fish will do, with haddock being the closest match.

INSTEAD OF SULTAN IBRAHIM, TRY RED MULLET: The royal name indicates how highly prized these fish are, for their delicate flesh and sweet flavor reminiscent of prawns or shrimp. Often served whole and pan-fried, crispy red mullets are the substitute and a great addition to your mezze table.

INSTEAD OF MUSHT, TRY PORGY: Musht is plentiful in the Sea of Galilee. In the Gospels of the Bible, it appears in the 'Feeding of the 5,000,' or Jesus' miracle of 'The Five Loaves and Two Fishes'. When I came to New York, I looked for a fish that was the most visually similar and found the mild, white porgy fish to be it.

AND EMBRACE SMALL BAIT: Anchovies and sardines tend to get a bad rap. But there's a whole lot to love about these small sea creatures. They absolutely brim with intense, maritime flavor, and because they're so delicate, they can often be enjoyed bones and all, making them a good source of calcium. You'd be hard-pressed to find a better source of omega-3s, and they remain largely sustainable at a time when other species are becoming dangerously overfished. My father had us eating sardines once a week for their nutritional benefit!

GRILLED FISH KEBABS

A friend of mine recently brought in three huge striped bass caught fresh from the waters of Long Island, New York, and I immediately had the idea for these kebabs. This mild-flavoured fish is a sustainable choice and marinating adds layer upon layer of flavour while keeping the dish light and healthy. **MAKES 5 SERVINGS**

2.3kg firm, thick fish fillets (preferably a sustainable species) such as bass, mahi mahi, or swordfish

1 tablespoon sea salt

1 teaspoon freshly ground black pepper

1 teaspoon ground coriander

1 teaspoon ground cumin

15g finely chopped fresh coriander

6 cloves garlic, finely diced

½ teaspoon ground fennel (optional)

120ml olive oil

Juice of 3 lemons

1 tablespoon finely chopped fresh dill

1 tablespoon Hot Pepper Paste (page 212; optional)

30 cherry tomatoes, red or yellow or a mix

10 skewers (soaked in water for 10–30 minutes if using wooden skewers)

Rocket, grilled fresh pineapple rings, lemon slices, and Tarator Sauce (page 210), for serving

Cut the fish into 2.5 x 5cm cubes and put them in a large bowl. In a small bowl, whisk together the salt, black pepper, coriander, cumin, coriander, garlic and fennel, if using, and rub it all over the fish. Leave to sit for 10 minutes. In a separate bowl, whisk the oil, lemon juice, dill and pepper paste, if using, pour over the fish, turn to evenly coat, and leave it to sit for 1 hour in the refrigerator.

Heat a grill or griddle pan to a medium heat and rub with vegetable oil, or preheat the broiler.

Thread about 5 pieces of fish on each skewer with a cherry tomato between each and place on the barbecue or under the grill for about 8 minutes, until cooked through. Serve on a bed of rocket with grilled pineapple rings, lemon slices, and Tarator Sauce.

MOROCCAN-STYLE STUFFED SARDINES

Whenever I interview someone for a position at the restaurant, the first thing I ask them to do is make something from their own country. A Moroccan cook taught me this wonderful way to prepare fresh sardines. Needless to say, that person got the job! If you don't think you like sardines, it's probably because you've only had them from a tin. When they're fresh, they are sweet, not at all fishy tasting, and succulent. These stuffed sardines can either be pan-fried or grilled; I've given options for both. **MAKES 6 SERVINGS AS A MAIN DISH OR 12 AS A MEZZE**

24 whole fresh sardines (not tinned)

8 cloves garlic

1 long hot or poblano chilli, chopped

15g chopped fresh coriander

2 tablespoons Hot Pepper Paste (page 212)

1 tablespoon pomegranate molasses

4 tablespoons olive oil, plus more for cooking

Juice of 2 lemons

1 teaspoon ground cumin

1 tablespoon ground coriander

Sea salt and freshly ground black pepper

Baby rocket, fresh lemon juice, and shredded
    red onion, for serving

Take the heads off 12 of the sardines by slicing down behind the gills with a sharp knife, leaving the tails intact. Cut the bellies off all 24 sardines from head to tail, going as deep as you can without slicing all the way through the fish. Remove the backbones by pulling them gently away from the flesh. Press down on the backs of each sardine gently, so that each lays flat.

Place the remaining ingredients into a pestle and mortar or food processor and crush into a paste. Spread 1 tablespoon of the paste on the cut-open belly of each sardine. Sandwich the sardines by placing one head-on fish on top of one headless fish, with the paste in the centre (for 12 sandwiched sardines total). Thinly smear the outsides of each sandwich with the paste, coating them completely.

Drizzle the sardines with olive oil and toss to coat. Heat a charcoal grill or cast-iron griddle pan to medium-high. Add the sardines and cook for 4–5 minutes on one side. Turn over, and cook on the other side for 3 minutes, until grill marks appear on the fish.

To serve, place the fish on a bed of baby rocket and sprinkle with lemon juice and shredded red onion.

AUNT UM SAMI'S BAKED FISH KIBBEH

Growing up in Nazareth, we seldom ate red meat on Friday. The cafeteria at my elementary school would frequently serve lentil pilaf, or *mujadara*, which grew monotonous week after week. After school, my cousin Aida would take me to her house, where my aunt Um Sami would feed us her delicious fish kibbeh. Hers was the only other cooking my mother really respected. And since Um Sami was on a first-name basis with the local fishermen, she always used the freshest catch. A few summers ago, my family and I were on our annual deep-sea-fishing trip from Montauk Point, New York; we caught an enormous amount of fish, and my aunt's recipe came to mind all these years later. I settled on using grouper for the outer shell and striped bass for the stuffing. I like to serve this dish with fattoush.

MAKES 12–14 SERVINGS

SPICE MIX

2 tablespoons sea salt

3 tablespoons ground allspice

1 tablespoon ground cumin

1 tablespoon freshly ground black pepper

½ teaspoon ground cinnamon

¼ teaspoon ground nutmeg

1½ teaspoons ground marjoram

ZESTS

Zest of 1 lemon

Zest of 1 lime

Zest of 1 orange

OUTER LAYER

1.35kg skinless grouper (or haddock) fillets

½ white onion, chopped

450g fine bulgar wheat, soaked in enough cold water to cover for 30 minutes

2 tablespoons Hot Pepper Paste (page 212; optional)

STUFFING

Sea salt

1.35kg striped bass or another flaky fish fillet (such as sea bass), cut into 2.5cm cubes

240ml vegetable oil

120ml olive oil, plus more for greasing

3 white onions, diced

4 shallots, diced

15g chopped fresh coriander

80g flaked almonds, toasted

65g pine nuts or 50g walnuts, toasted

2 tablespoons pomegranate or grape molasses

3 tablespoons fresh lemon juice

Fattoush (page 78), for serving

Make the spice mix and zest mix: In a small bowl, whisk together all the spices. In a separate bowl, mix the zests.

Make the outer layer: Put the grouper and white onion in a food processor and process to a paste consistency. Place in a bowl with the soaked bulgar and stir to combine. Add half of the spice mix, half of the zest mix, and the hot pepper paste, if using, and combine well. Dip your hands into a bowl of ice water to moisten and knead the mixture between your hands to form it into a dough. Cover and refrigerate while you make the stuffing.

Make the stuffing: Sprinkle ½ teaspoon of the remaining spice mix and a pinch of salt onto the striped bass. Heat the vegetable oil in a large frying pan over a medium heat. Working in batches if necessary, sear the fish, stirring occasionally, until lightly browned on all sides. Place on a kitchen paper–lined plate to drain.

Remove the vegetable oil from the pan and add the olive oil. Heat over a medium heat, add the onions and shallots, and cook until lightly browned, about 4 minutes. Add the coriander and cook for 2-3 minutes, until wilted. Add the fish cubes, almonds, pine nuts, the reserved zest, the remaining spice mix, the pomegranate molasses and lemon juice. Stir well, remove from the heat and season with salt. Spread on a baking tray and cool to room temperature.

Make the kibbeh: Preheat the oven to 180°C/gas mark 4. Coat the bottom and sides of a 23 x 33cm glass baking dish with olive oil.

Remove the outer layer mixture from the refrigerator and divide it in half. Evenly line the bottom and sides of the dish with one half. Top with the stuffing, spreading it into an even layer. Top with the remaining shell mixture, moistening your hands as needed with ice water, to press it into a flat, even layer. Score the kibbeh into triangles, rectangles, or squares, making sure to cut only through the top layer of shell.

Bake for 30–40 minutes, until golden brown. Let cool for 15 minutes (so portions hold their shape when served).

GRILLED SESAME PRAWNS

It's no secret that the Middle East is a land of tahini lovers. Tahini works in mezze, stews and sauces and goes with every kind of meat or vegetable. For delicately flavoured and textured seafood, the paste needs to be applied in just the right amount. I like to throw on a few skewers of vegetables as a side dish while the grill is fired up (but don't place them on the same skewers as the prawns, as they will cook at different rates). Some of my favourites are peppers, baby onions, and tiny cherry tomatoes. **MAKES 8 SERVINGS**

MARINADE

225g tahini

3 tablespoons sesame oil

1 tablespoon finely chopped garlic

1 shallot, finely chopped

1 poblano chilli, finely chopped

1 tablespoon Hot Pepper Paste (page 212)

1½ teaspoons ground cumin

1½ teaspoons ground coriander

1 tablespoon freshly ground black pepper

15g chopped fresh basil

15g chopped fresh coriander

Pinch of sea salt

1 tablespoon grated fresh ginger

40–50 raw prawns (any size), peeled and deveined

Skewers (if using wooden skewers, soak in
        water for 10–30 minutes)

240ml fresh lemon juice

Chopped fresh flat-leaf parsley, for garnish

Toasted sesame seeds, for garnish

Marinate the prawns: In a large bowl or food processor, combine the tahini, sesame oil, garlic, shallot, chilli, hot pepper paste, cumin, coriander, black pepper, basil, coriander and salt and whisk or process until combined. Stir in the ginger. Gently toss half of the marinade with the prawns. Cover with clingfilm and marinate in the refrigerator for 30 minutes.

Make the dipping sauce: Place the remaining marinade in a blender, add the lemon juice, and blend until smooth, adding add a few drops of water if it's too thick. Chill in the refrigerator in a separate container until ready to serve.

Thread the prawns onto the skewers. Lightly oil the grill or griddle pan and cook the prawns, turning once, until just cooked through, 4–5 minutes total. Remove to a plate, garnish with parsley and toasted sesame seeds and serve with the dipping sauce alongside.

CHRISTMAS SEAFOOD ARTICHOKES

What was once a special event for holiday meals before I opened Tanoreen has become one of the most highly requested dishes at the restaurant. An artichoke served whole in its flower-like state is a show-stopper, but when you stuff those emerald leaves with a bounty of fresh crab, prawns, and clams, it soars to new heights.

These elegant artichokes are suited to be enjoyed communally, with family and friends gathered around the table together pulling apart the seafood-mounded, nature-made spoons. Alternatively, they can be split in half for a bountiful plated appetiser or even offered as the main event, with each diner receiving his or her own artichoke with rice pilaf or crusty warmed bread alongside.

Not a fan of clams? Prefer lobster to crab or scallops to prawns? You can substitute any seafood you like, as long as the measurements stay the same. Want to go gluten-free? Go on and remove the breadcrumbs, and add an extra egg white as a binder. **MAKES 4 LARGE ARTICHOKES**

6 tablespoons olive oil, plus more for drizzling

2 tablespoons crushed garlic

1 long hot or other chilli, finely diced (optional)

450g extra large raw prawns, peeled, deveined, and finely chopped

225g small raw clams, shucked (optional)

1 tablespoon ground coriander

1 tablespoon freshly ground black pepper

Sea salt

300g cooked white crabmeat

125g unseasoned breadcrumbs (I prefer panko)

¼ cup Coriander-Basil Pesto (page 216) or shop-bought pesto

1 tablespoon finely chopped fresh coriander

Juice of 2 lemons, plus 4 tablespoons

Zest of 1 lime

1 large egg white, beaten

4 large artichokes, cleaned and cooked (see 172)

480ml clam juice (available online)

240ml chicken or vegetable stock

Preheat the oven to 200°C/gas mark 6.

Heat the oil in a large frying pan over a medium heat. Add the garlic and chilli, if using, and cook until aromatic but not coloured, about 1 minute. Add the prawns and clams, if using, and cook until cooked through but not rubbery, about 2 minutes. Add the coriander and black pepper and season with salt. Stir to combine, then remove from the heat and cool.

In a large bowl, combine the crabmeat, breadcrumbs, pesto, coriander, juice of 2 lemons, lime zest, egg white, and prawns mixture. Season with salt and stir to thoroughly combine.

Fill the centre of the artichokes with the stuffing. Starting from the outside, place a teaspoon or so of stuffing behind each of the leaves so that the whole artichoke opens like a flower. Nestle the artichokes closely together in a baking dish and drizzle with oil. Top with whatever remains of the stuffing.

In a medium bowl, whisk together the clam juice, chicken stock and 4 tablespoons lemon juice and drizzle it evenly over the artichokes, allowing it to drip to the bottom of the baking dish. Cover the dish tightly with a sheet of parchment paper followed by aluminium foil and bake for 10 minutes. Reduce the oven temperature to 180°C/gas mark 4 and bake for another 15 minutes. Remove the foil and parchment paper and bake until the breadcrumbs are golden brown, 3–5 minutes more.

MORE THAN A STUFFING: The seafood stuffing in this recipe can also work as a topping for pasta. Simply heat it up with a drizzle of extra virgin olive oil and toss together with cooked spaghetti. It can also top crostini to make a beautiful appetiser. You might also like to serve it cold as a seafood salad. So if you have any extra stuffing left over, make sure it works double-duty for you.

How to Prepare Artichokes

Bring a large pan of water to the boil and add a generous handful of salt.

Use a sharp knife to cut the stems off the artichokes so they sit flat. Lay each artichoke on its side and cut off the top 2.5cm or so to reveal the fuzzy choke. Use kitchen shears to snip the top 5cm or so off each leaf to remove the prickly barbs.

Using a melon baller or teaspoon, dig out the chokes (including the feathery fronds) so the artichokes are clean, empty, and ready to be stuffed.

Add the artichokes to the boiling water and return to the boil. Reduce the heat, cover, and simmer for 20–30 minutes, until you can easily pull a leaf from the centre of the artichokes.

Transfer the artichokes to a bowl filled with water and ice to stop the cooking and to cool them enough to handle and stuff. Drain and pat dry with kitchen paper.

TOP: Cutting off the artichoke stem; using a spoon to remove the choke. **BOTTOM:** Adding the stuffing; closing the flower back together.

SWEETS

THE SENTIMENTALITY OF SWEETS

When I was growing up in Nazareth, there wasn't a restaurant culture, as almost all our meals were made at home. The same was true for desserts — while there were bakeries, they were limited to bread and just a few pastries.

There's a deep sense of tradition surrounding cookies, cakes and more elaborate confections in the Middle East. Some sweets were prepared for daily enjoyment, while others would appear mostly at special events or around the holidays. I still vividly remember my mother's kitchen smelling of rose water and orange blossom water when she would make Easter cookies and the sight of mounds of dates being kneaded with cinnamon before being stuffed into crumbly semolina cookies.

So although baking is a more scientific endeavour than cooking, it remains sentimental to me as well. The desserts in this chapter evoke that feeling of ritual and nostalgia, while at the same time veering slightly from tradition. I believe that you can transform time-honoured dishes while maintaining their integrity, such as with my Chocolate Baklava (page 179) and Mabroosheh (page 180). And sometimes I'll reimagine the use of an ingredient entirely — Honey-Cured Aubergine (page 182) will be the talk of your table.

When it comes to baking, I rely heavily on nuts and spices, natural sweeteners like honey and carob molasses and plenty of fresh and preserved fruit. At my restaurant, I've increasingly noticed that while people want to indulge in a toothsome dessert after a nice meal (who doesn't?), they also want the experience to be as guilt-free as possible. So from Triple Almond Cake (page 187) that's made entirely without gluten, to cakes moistened with carrots and butternut squash, the following recipes were designed to be unexpectedly wholesome yet scrumptious enough to charm even the most committed sweet tooth.

OLIVE OIL, BUTTERNUT SQUASH & CARROT CAKE

I first tasted carrot cake when my husband and I moved into our first home in New York and a neighbour generously brought one to us. I was fascinated with the idea of making cake with vegetables, which is how I came up with my version of carrot cake using butternut squash and olive oil instead of butter and studded it with plump raisins. It's as guilt-free as a cake can get. I enjoy this cake all on its own, with a cup of tea or coffee in the morning. **MAKES ABOUT 12 SERVINGS**

260g plain flour, plus more for dusting

1 teaspoon sea salt

2 teaspoons bicarbonate of soda

1 tablespoon ground cinnamon

1 teaspoon ground allspice

4 medium eggs

400g brown sugar

240g mild olive oil

150ml apple juice

70g raisins

50g chopped walnuts

35g unsweetened shredded coconut

540g grated carrots, squeezed to remove excess moisture

125g grated butternut squash, squeezed to remove excess moisture

Preheat the oven to 150°C/gas mark 2. Flour a 23 x 33cm cake tin.

Sift the flour, salt, bicarbonate of soda, cinnamon and allspice into a large bowl and set aside.

In the bowl of a stand mixer fitted with the whisk attachment, combine the eggs, brown sugar, oil and apple juice and beat for 2 minutes. Add the dry ingredients and beat for 3 minutes. Add the raisins, walnuts and coconut and beat for 2 minutes. Using a rubber spatula, fold in the carrots and squash.

Add the batter to the prepared pan and bake for 45–60 minutes, until a toothpick inserted into the centre of the cake comes out clean. Let cool in the tin set on a wire rack until the cake is just warm or room temperature. Cut into squares to serve. Leftovers will keep, covered in clingfilm, at room temperature for up to 2 days.

Carrots and butternut squash
are simply bursting with natural sugar and moisture, making them ideal additions to baked goods like cake (not merely a clever way of sneaking vegetables into your kids' – or perhaps your own – food).

CHOCOLATE BAKLAVA

With its delicate, crispy, syrup-soaked layers of buttered filo and its spiced, crunchy, nutty middle layer, this iconic dessert known around the world needs little introduction. So imagine how incredible it is with one simple, innovative tweak — a thick layer of dark, melted chocolate running through the centre. Feeling especially sinful? You can even splash a shot of cocoa- or hazelnut-flavoured liqueur in with the chocolate layer. **MAKES ABOUT 24 SERVINGS**

Butter, for greasing

630g chopped walnuts

130g chopped hazelnuts

60g chopped pistachios

1 teaspoon ground cinnamon

½ teaspoon ground allspice

Pinch of ground cloves

Pinch of freshly grated nutmeg

280g honey or 140g icing sugar

2 tablespoons orange blossom water

2 tablespoons rose water

450g frozen filo dough, defrosted

450g unsalted butter or ghee, melted and cooled

450g dark chocolate, finely grated
    or melted

BLOSSOM-SCENTED SIMPLE SYRUP

400g sugar

1 tablespoon rose water

2 tablespoons orange blossom water

3 drops of fresh lemon juice

Preheat the oven to 150°C/gas mark 2. Generously butter a 23 x 33cm baking dish.

In a large bowl, mix together the walnuts, hazelnuts, pistachios, cinnamon, allspice, cloves and nutmeg. Stir in the honey, orange blossom water and rose water.

Keep the stack of filo sheets covered with a dampened tea towel so they don't dry out while you work. Place one sheet of filo into the dish, trimming or folding over the edges if necessary and brush evenly with melted butter. Repeat with half of the filo sheets, buttering each sheet.

Spread the nut mixture evenly over the top layer of filo. Lay down another sheet of filo, lightly brush with butter, and top with the chocolate. Top with the remaining sheets of filo, buttering each sheet.

Make the syrup: Combine all the ingredients with 720ml water in a small saucepan. Bring to a simmer over a medium heat and simmer, stirring occasionally, until the sugar is dissolved. Place in the refrigerator to cool. (The syrup will keep, stored in an airtight container in the refrigerator for up to 2 weeks.)

Score the baklava by cutting 4cm-wide strips into the pastry (only go as far as the nut layer), then cutting diagonally to form diamond shapes. Bake for 1–1½ hours, until golden and flaky. Evenly cover with 480ml of the chilled syrup.

Cut along the score marks to serve. To store, cover the pan with clingfilm; the baklava will keep in a cool, dark place for up to 1 week.

JAM & TAHINI SQUARES

MABROOSHEH

When I was younger, seasonal fresh fruit and berry jams were made towards the end of the hot Nazareth summer for peak sweetness. And to utilise these jewel-coloured jars of preserves, my mother would frequently bake mabroosheh. The name comes from the verb *barish* (to grate), which is what we do with the dough that tops a cookie-like yellow cake base and vibrant jammy centre. It's the perfect accompaniment to an afternoon cup of tea. To keep it from being too traditional, here I've added tahini, which contributes added depth and an extra layer of nutty richness to the cake. **MAKES ABOUT 12 SERVINGS**

Butter, for greasing

4 medium eggs, beaten

225g unsalted butter, melted,
    or 150ml olive oil

225g tahini

300g sugar

2 tablespoons vanilla extract

2 tablespoons fruit liqueur (optional;
    use the same flavour as your jam)

260g plain flour, plus more for dusting

½ teaspoon baking powder

290g sugar-free jam or preserves

Preheat the oven to 150°C/gas mark 2. Grease and lightly flour a 23 x 33cm baking dish.

In a large bowl, whisk together the eggs, butter and tahini. Add the sugar, vanilla, liqueur, if using, flour and baking powder and fold it into a stiff dough.

Take two-thirds of the dough and evenly spread it along the bottom of the dish. Cover the dough with the jam. Using the largest holes of a hand or box grater, grate the remaining dough over the top of the jam. Cover the dish with aluminium foil and bake until golden brown, 35–40 minutes.

Cut into squares to serve. To store, cover the dish with clingfilm and place in the refrigerator, where it will keep for up to 1 week.

PISTACHIO-STUFFED CHOCOLATE-DIPPED FRUIT

I first ate these in Amman, Jordan, at a fantastic patisserie my sister frequents. Now whenever family from Amman visits us in New York, they know what to bring. I have re-created them here with a few additional flourishes that I think make all the difference — I plump the dried figs, dates and apricots before I dip them to create a happy medium between fresh and dried. These are great for holidays, dinner parties or simply as a middle-of-the-week pick-me-up. Who doesn't love chocolate? **MAKES 1.35KG**

450g dried figs
450g dried apricots
450g pitted dried dates
450g whole shelled pistachios
450g high-quality chocolate (I like plain), melted

Bring a pan of water to a simmer, add the figs and apricots and cook for 5 minutes, then add the dates and cook for an additional 5 minutes, until plumped. Carefully remove the fruit with a slotted spoon and gently pat dry with kitchen paper. Set aside to cool.

Using your fingers or a knife, slit the fruit along one side so they resemble partially opened clamshells. Stuff the cavities with 3 or 4 pistachios and press the edges with your fingers to close. Set in a sieve over a large bowl and leave in the refrigerator or on the counter overnight.

The next day, coat the fruit on all sides with the melted chocolate and place in a single layer on parchment paper. Place in the refrigerator to set before serving. The fruit will keep in an airtight container in the refrigerator for up to 1 week.

HONEY-CURED AUBERGINE

This unique showstopper of a dessert is something I adapted from a Turkish treat my mother learned to make many years ago. It's made from whole baby aubergines cooked in syrup and is bursting with citrus, ginger and warm, sweet spices. This sweet yet savoury dish is a true conversation starter. Enjoy solo, or serve atop cottage cheese, ricotta cheese or vanilla ice cream. **MAKES ABOUT 6 SERVINGS**

1.35kg baby aubergines, no longer than 7.5cm each

225g walnut halves

400g sugar

2 tablespoons orange blossom water

2 tablespoons rose water

10 whole cloves

Zest of 1 orange, cut into 2.5cm-long pieces

240ml fresh orange juice

2.5cm piece fresh ginger, peeled and thinly sliced

140g honey

Poke a few holes in the flesh of the aubergine with a toothpick. Do not remove the crowns or peel away the skin.

Bring a large saucepan of water to the boil (make sure there's enough water to fully cover the aubergines). Drop the aubergines in the water and cover with a heatproof plate so they remain fully submerged. Simmer for 7–10 minutes, until the aubergines are just tender, but still hold their shape. Strain and gently press the aubergines with a tea towel so they release their surplus water.

Using a small knife, cut a slit in one side of each aubergine, being careful not to slice all the way through. Push two walnut halves into each slit.

In a large saucepan, combine the sugar, orange blossom water, rose water, the remaining walnuts and 960ml water. Bring to the boil over a medium heat and boil for 10 minutes, stirring occasionally. Add the cloves, orange peel, orange juice, ginger and stuffed aubergines, return to the boil, and boil until the liquid reduces by about half, about 10 minutes. Turn off the heat and add the honey. Gently stir with a rubber spatula, so the honey evenly coats the aubergine.

Place one layer of aubergine into a deep jar or container with the walnuts facing up. Spoon a layer of syrup on top, making sure to include some of the zest, ginger, walnuts and cloves. Continue layering aubergines with syrup, finishing with about 2.5cm of syrup at the top of the jar.

Let the contents of the jar cool completely, then cover and refrigerate until ready to serve.

NOTE: Can't imagine eating aubergine for dessert? This recipe is just as delicious made with fresh dates.

SWIRLED MOLASSES PUDDING

KHABSAH

Loosely translated as 'mixed mess', *khabsah* is one of the oldest and simplest desserts found throughout the Levant. This swirled pudding uses pantry items that traditionally every family would have on hand: milk from a local cow or goat and carob molasses. The molasses would be extracted from readily available carob pods by cooking, reducing and straining the fruit and it would be stored away to be used as a sweetener throughout the year.

My update on the time-honoured sweet? Making it even more of a khabsah by adding more fun flourishes. You can flavour it with mastic, a widely used aromatic resin from the sap of a Mediterranean tree in the cashew family that imparts a pine-like, almost cedar flavour. I love shredded sweetened coconut as a topping, and if you want to get really fancy, you can also add ripe seasonal fruit such as black cherries, apricot preserves or Stone Fruit Compote. **MAKES 8–10 SERVINGS**

MILK PUDDING

6 tablespoons cornflour

1.4 litres milk

140g honey

1 tablespoon rose water

¼ teaspoon mastic (optional)

CAROB PUDDING

4 tablespoons cornflour

960ml boiling water

6 tablespoons carob molasses, or to taste (see note)

Stone Fruit Compote (opposite), roasted nuts, such as pistachios, and/or shredded sweetened coconut, for serving (optional)

Make the milk pudding: In a small bowl, whisk the cornflour into just enough of the milk (about 4 tablespoons) to make a paste. Pour the rest of the milk into a medium saucepan along with the honey, rose water and mastic. Whisk to combine and bring to the boil over a medium heat. Whisk in the cornflour paste and cook, stirring frequently, until the pudding has thickened and the spoon can leave tracks in the pudding. Pour into a lightly greased 23 x 33cm baking dish and set aside.

Make the carob pudding: In a small bowl, whisk the cornflour into just enough of the boiling water (about 4 tablespoons) to make a paste. Pour the rest of the water into a medium saucepan along with the carob molasses. Whisk to combine and bring to the boil over a medium heat. Whisk in the cornflour paste and cook, stirring frequently, until the pudding has thickened and the spoon can leave tracks in the pudding. Drizzle an even layer over the milk pudding and swirl the two together using a fork or butter knife (do not combine them completely). Cover the surface of the pudding directly with clingfilm so it doesn't develop a skin and put in the refrigerator or allow to cool at room temperature. Serve unadorned or with stone fruit compote, nuts and/or coconut. Leftovers can be covered tightly with clingfilm and stored in the refrigerator, where they will keep for up to 3 days.

NOTE: Grape or pomegranate molasses are acceptable substitutes for the carob molasses, but are a bit more lemony, so you might want to add a bit of honey if you use one of them.

STONE FRUIT COMPOTE

This age-old dessert is simple and makes good use of ripe fruit you have sitting around. There are so many ways to enjoy it. Try spooning it on top of ice cream or yogurt and sprinkle it with pistachios, walnuts or fresh shredded coconut. You can also use the compote in a crumble, served warm with fresh whipped cream. It keeps for days in the refrigerator, making it a beautiful ready-to-eat snack. **MAKES 6–8 SERVINGS**

2 quince, peeled, stoned and cut into 1.25cm squares
    (can also use apples or pears)
10 apricots, halved and stoned
4 nectarines, stoned and sliced
10 whole cloves
2.5cm piece fresh ginger, thinly sliced
Zest of 1 orange
Juice of 2 oranges, plus more if needed
3 tablespoons honey
1 teaspoon vanilla extract
1 tablespoon Grand Marnier
1 tablespoon raspberry liqueur

Combine all the ingredients in a large saucepan and set over a low heat. Cook, stirring occasionally, until the quince is softened, about 30 minutes, adding a little more orange juice if it starts getting dry. Cool completely, then refrigerate until chilled before serving. The compote will keep for up to 1 week, covered in the refrigerator.

It's easy to tire of apples and pears during the long, cold slog of fall and winter, which is why I urge you to take a chance on quince. Granted, you can't eat the fruit out of hand (their bitter, woody flesh renders them inedible raw), but magic happens when you add heat. Braised, boiled or roasted, quince releases a floral, vanilla aroma that's more intoxicating than the finest perfume. And the flavour (think of pear on vacation in the tropics) is enchanting too, making quince as appealing scooped on top of ice cream as it is simmered in a spicy stew with meat.

TRIPLE ALMOND CAKE

If you are a fan of almonds, this cake is for you. It not only utilises ground almonds, but marzipan (almond paste) appears both in the batter and as an intensely rich middle layer and it finishes with a scattering of sliced almonds. Marzipan is a sweet concentrated almond paste used in many confections and chocolates. For my personal taste, it can be a bit too sweet, which is why I prefer to make my own, so that I can control how much sugar is added.

    This makes a wonderful spring holiday dessert and is excellent with coffee. Try serving it accompanied with Stone Fruit Compote recipe (page 185). **MAKES ABOUT 12 SERVINGS**

Butter, for greasing

Plain flour, for dusting

500g marzipan, homemade (recipe follows) or shop-bought

170g unsalted butter, at room temperature

6 medium eggs

3 tablespoons rose water

200g ground almonds

1½ tablespoons baking powder

200g granulated sugar

Pinch of sea salt

Zest of 1 lemon

Sliced almonds and icing sugar, for serving

Preheat the oven to 150°C/gas mark 2. Grease a Bundt pan and dust lightly with flour, shaking out any excess.

    Place half of the marzipan into the bowl of a stand mixer, fitted with the whisk attachment. Add the butter and mix until it becomes foamy. Carefully add the eggs one at a time as you mix. Add the rose water and beat until fluffy, 3–5 minutes. In another bowl, whisk together the ground almonds, baking powder, sugar, salt and lemon zest. Gradually add these dry ingredients to the butter mixture and mix for 5 minutes.

    Pour half of the batter into the prepared pan. Evenly top with the remaining half of the marzipan by breaking off bits and scattering them over the batter (they will sink into the batter). Top with the rest of the batter. Bake for about 1 hour, until the cake springs back when pressed. Remove the cake from the oven and let it cool in the pan for a few minutes. Run a thick knife around the edge of the cake to make sure it has released from the pan, then flip it onto a plate. Let the cake cool completely. Serve at room temperature, sprinkled with sliced almonds and dusted with icing sugar.

MARZIPAN

500g blanched flaked or whole raw almonds

6 tablespoons honey, or more to taste

2 tablespoons vanilla extract

1 tablespoon Amaretto liqueur (optional)

1 tablespoon Frangelico liqueur (optional)

In a food processor, process the almonds until ground and clumpy. Add the honey, vanilla and Amaretto and Frangelico, if using. Process until the mixture is the consistency of dough. You can make the marzipan in advance; it will keep, covered in the refrigerator, for up to 1 week.

CARAWAY PUDDING
WITH NUTS AND HONEY

CARAWIA

Traditionally this dish is made after a child is born. The name *carawia* is used in our region of the Galilee, although you can find it as *moghli* in other areas of the Levant. When I had my second child, my mother-in-law made it for me. It was delicious and not too sweet, the kind of dessert that can satisfy a craving without being overindulgent. And after giving birth, I really wanted to lose some baby weight! The pudding is filling and inexpensive, made with little more than rice flour, water and caraway seeds, with honey, nuts and fruit to make it sweet. Not that further persuasion is needed, but it is dairy-free, gluten-free, and incredibly low in fat! And it rhymes with my name. **MAKES 6 SERVINGS**

2.1 litres water or milk

1½ teaspoons vanilla extract

½ teaspoon ground cinnamon

Pinch of ground cloves

Pinch of freshly grated nutmeg

2½ tablespoons ground caraway seeds

1¼ tablespoons ground fennel seeds

8 heaped teaspoons rice flour

140g honey

3 tablespoons maple syrup

Toppings of your choice, such as pomegranate seeds, walnuts, pistachios, coconut, raisins, liquorice, maple syrup, or cinnamon sugar

In a large saucepan, bring the water or milk to the boil over a medium heat and add the vanilla, cinnamon, cloves, nutmeg, caraway seeds and fennel seeds. Gradually add the rice flour, whisking constantly so it doesn't clump. Reduce the heat and simmer, stirring frequently, until the pudding thickens, 12–15 minutes. Stir in the honey and maple syrup and add your choice of toppings. You may serve the pudding warm, or refrigerate it until chilled, in a large glass bowl or individual ramekins. The pudding will keep, covered with clingfilm, in the refrigerator for up to 1 week.

While dessert can be a dirty word to dieters, this pudding is essentially a collection of virtuous ingredients. Caraway is a tiny seed that packs a lot of punch: it's chock-full of minerals, vitamins and antioxidants and is an excellent digestive, making carawia the perfect finale to a big meal.

CRISPY WALNUT-STUFFED CRESCENTS

KATAYEF

These crispy, crescent-shaped desserts are traditionally served during the month of Ramadan. And while my family and many of my guests are not Muslim, we can't get enough of these fried, stuffed pancakes, which — whether filled with cheese or a spiced walnut mixture — are an incredible sensory experience. They're at once sweet, crunchy, chewy and bright with the flavours of orange blossom and cinnamon. Just make sure to eat them as soon as they're made, as that wonderful contrast of tastes and textures is at its peak just after the fragrant syrup bath. **MAKES ABOUT 16 PANCAKES**

PANCAKES
165g plain flour
½ teaspoon active dried yeast
1 teaspoon baking powder
1 tablespoon granulated sugar
Pinch of sea salt
240ml milk
Butter, for griddling

WALNUT STUFFING
210g chopped walnuts
35g unsweetened shredded coconut
70g raisins
½ teaspoon ground cinnamon
Pinch of freshly grated nutmeg
Pinch of ground cloves
2 tablespoons orange blossom water
3 tablespoons icing sugar or honey

720ml vegetable oil, for frying
Blossom-Scented Simple Syrup (see page 179),
    for serving

Make the pancakes: In a large bowl, whisk together the flour, yeast, baking powder, sugar and salt. Add the milk and whisk to combine. Cover with a moist tea towel and set aside to rise for 1 hour.

Heat a large frying pan or pancake griddle and grease it with butter. Using a ladle, add batter to the griddle to make 12.5cm pancakes. Cook on one side only, until you see the sides drying and holes bubbling up in the centre. As the pancakes are cooked, transfer them to a baking tray using a spatula, griddled side facing down. Repeat with the remaining batter.

Make the stuffing: In a medium bowl, combine all the stuffing ingredients. Place a spoonful of the mixture onto each pancake and fold over to make half circles. Pinch the crescents closed around the rim.

Fry the pancakes: In a medium saucepan, heat the oil until very hot, but not smoking. Add as many pancakes as you can without crowding the pan and fry until golden brown and crispy on all sides, about 2 minutes on each side. Drizzle with the simple syrup and serve immediately.

LAYERED CUSTARD & NUT CRUMBLE

KSHTALEIA

Every culture has recipes that make use of leftovers, and this is one of ours. The crust is traditionally formed from bits of stale bread, though you could easily make this gluten-free by swapping additional ground nuts for the breadcrumbs. The delicate, flowery pudding could be served all on its own, finished with a drizzle of honey and a pinch of cinnamon. **MAKES ABOUT 12 SERVINGS**

Butter, for greasing

PUDDING
1.9 litres milk
2 tablespoons rose water
2 tablespoons orange blossom water
140g icing sugar or 280g honey
1 teaspoon vanilla extract
1 teaspoon mastic (optional)
120g rice flour

CRUST
45g panko breadcrumbs
80g unseasoned standard breadcrumbs
105g chopped walnuts
120g chopped almonds
340g unsalted butter, melted
1 tablespoon vanilla extract
½ teaspoon ground cinnamon

290g jam of your choice
250ml Blossom-Scented Simple Syrup
    (page 179), to serve

Preheat the oven to 150°C/gas mark 2. Grease a 23 x 33cm baking dish with butter.

In a large saucepan, bring the milk to a simmer over a medium heat. Add the rose water, orange blossom water, icing sugar, vanilla and mastic, if using. Slowly add the rice flour, stirring all the while. Cook until the pudding begins to thicken and a whisk leaves tracks in the mixture. Spread evenly on a baking tray to cool.

Make the crust: In a large bowl, combine the panko, standard breadcrumbs, walnuts and almonds. Add the melted butter, vanilla and cinnamon, working the mixture with your hands. Spread half of the breadcrumb mixture over the bottom of the prepared dish. Using a spatula, pack it down evenly and firmly. Spread the pudding mixture over the top, then spread the jam over the pudding. Sprinkle the remaining bread mixture on top of the jam and press it down.

Bake until the crust is golden brown. Pour the simple syrup over the top and let it cool for a few minutes. To serve, cut into squares. The kshtaleia is equally good cold. To store, cover the dish with clingfilm and place in the refrigerator, where it will keep for up to 1 week.

BUTTER COOKIE SANDWICHES

GRAYBEH

This is my version of the incredibly popular Lebanese sugar cookie called *graybeh*, which I've enhanced with a touch of real vanilla bean seeds (not a traditional Middle Eastern ingredient), and made lighter by cutting down on the butter. Don't get me wrong, they still have plenty of butter, but you can actually taste the difference; these are so delicate they practically dissolve in your mouth. They also couldn't be simpler to bake and are the perfect accompaniment to a cup of coffee or tea. **MAKES ABOUT 3 DOZEN**

450g unsalted butter, at room temperature
200g icing sugar
Seeds from 1 vanilla pod
520g plain flour
290g jam or preserves (I like fig, quince or apricot)
100g ground pistachios (optional)

Preheat the oven to 150°C/gas mark 2.

Put the butter in the bowl of a stand mixer fitted with the whisk attachment. Start beating on low speed and gradually increase the speed to high. Beat until light and fluffy, about 3 minutes. Add the icing sugar and continue to beat until the mixture is foamy. Beat in the vanilla seeds. Add the flour a little at a time and beat until the dough holds together when pressed between your fingers.

Divide the dough in half and pat each half into a disc. Wrap in clingfilm and refrigerate until firm, about 1 hour.

Preheat the oven to 180°C. Grease two large baking trays or line with parchment paper.

On a lightly floured surface, roll one disc of dough out to a thickness of 0.5cm. Cut out circles using a 5cm round cookie cutter. Gather the scraps, roll out, cut and repeat until you've used all of the dough. Transfer to one of the prepared baking trays and place in the refrigerator to chill for 30 minutes.

Repeat the rolling and cutting process with the remaining disc of dough. Then use a smaller (no bigger than 2.5cm) cookie cutter or the wide end of a piping tip to make a cutout in the centre of each circle. (Discard the small cutout pieces.) Transfer the circles to the second prepared baking tray and place in the refrigerator to chill for 30 minutes.

Place both baking trays in the oven and bake for 8–10 minutes, until the edges of the cookies are just beginning to brown. Let the cookies cool for 5 minutes on the sheets, then roll in ground pistachios if desired, and transfer to a wire rack to cool completely.

To make the sandwiches, turn the cookies without holes flat-side up, and gently spread each with ½ teaspoon of jam. Top with the cut-out cookies, flat side down. Store in airtight containers for up to 1 week.

BEVERAGES

DRINK TO YOUR HEALTH

In a bygone era, free of refrigerators packed with unnaturally coloured and flavoured beverages, Middle Easterners made their own flavoured sharab (drinks). Hot, drawn-out summers provided reason enough to be innovative in producing a variety of juices and teas, many of which have been enjoyed now for centuries.

Egypt is known for hibiscus – a sweet, fragrant infusion made from handfuls of pink flowers. Jerusalem, for me, is associated with tamarind and date beverages sold on the street and poured over big blocks of ice. Syria is famous for its roses; in season, there are fields filled with thousands of bright red roses for making their signature sharab. And we the Palestinians (together with the Lebanese and other Mediterraneans) have counted citrus as our speciality. We'd squeeze fresh lemons, limes and oranges in summer and every kitchen would contain three bottles of concentrate during the winter for mixing with water and simple syrup and enjoying throughout the year.

As for hot drinks, the first written recipes on record hail from Iraq; mostly potions made with steeped herbs. That's because in ancient times herbs were used as medicine and while people throughout the Middle East eventually developed a taste for them, there's no doubt they still have curative properties.

Take aynar, a soothing cinnamon drink offered to new mothers right after giving birth. Or yansoun, heady with anise and excellent for calming the nerves. There are teas made with ginger, with turmeric, with chamomile. After thousands of years in practice, these treatments have ceased to be experimental. Put honey, ginger and orange peel in a pan and you're bound to feel better in the morning.

I continue to make all these drinks from another era. Yes, I play with them a bit, maybe add some cloves here or a vanilla pod there. I also borrowed inspiration from Mexican aguas frescas, which are diluted with water. It's a wonderful way of lightening up your drinks and cutting down on sugar (and stretching a some cash while you're at it).

ICED HIBISCUS TEA

KARKADEH

We have Egypt to thank for this striking caffeine-free magenta tea, made from the petals of dried roselle flowers (a species of hibiscus). Widely used to break the fast at Ramadan – thanks to its stomach-soothing abilities – the appeal of steeped hibiscus goes well beyond that, containing elements of sweet, tart and spicy (similar to mulled wine) that make for one perfectly balanced drink. **MAKES 3.8 LITRES**

8 tablespoons dried hibiscus flowers
2.85 litres boiling water
140g honey, or to taste

Put the hibiscus flowers in a large saucepan and add the boiling water. Let sit for 1 hour. Strain into a large jug, add the honey and whisk to dissolve the honey. Serve over ice.

ROSE WATER LEMONADE

Rose water is a tricky ingredient. One drop too much and you can go from breathing in an armful of flowers to swallowing a bottle of washing up liquid. Luckily, I've got the measurements for this exceptionally refreshing lemonade down to a science. You can be sure that it will refresh on the hottest, muggiest of summer days. **MAKES 3.8 LITRES**

480ml fresh lemon juice
350g sugar
3 tablespoons orange blossom water
2 tablespoons rose water
Lemon wedges and fresh mint leaves, to garnish

In a 4 litres jug, combine all the ingredients, except the garnishes, and stir until the sugar dissolves. Top off the jug with water. Serve in glasses over ice with lemon wedges and fresh mint leaves to garnish.

TAMARIND COOLER

This fruity refresher is a quintessential part of the street food scene in the Middle East. We would grab a cold glass along with za'atar flatbreads (page 33) and sesame seed cakes as a go-to snack after school. It hearkens back to pre-supermarket days, when 'concentrate' meant real fruit broken down with water and some sort of natural sweetener; no more, no less. But what it lacks in bells and whistles, it makes up for in pure, unadulterated flavour and is wondrous over ice on a sweltering summer day. Tamarind sharab is almost identical to the traditional Mexican tamarindo — each is beloved by and authentic to its culture, proof to me that food is our foremost cultural ambassador. **MAKES 950ML CONCENTRATE**

450g tamarind paste (pressed block of pulp and seeds, not concentrate)

140g honey, or to taste

1 tablespoon rose water

Halve the block of tamarind horizontally and vertically to make four equal squares. Place in a saucepan along with 480ml water and set over a medium heat. Use a wooden spoon to stir and break down the mixture until it melts and dissolves completely.

Set a fine-mesh sieve over a bowl or jug and press the paste through it using the back of a wooden spoon so the liquid falls into the container and the seeds and pulp stay in the strainer. Stir the rose water and honey into the liquid. This is your concentrate.

To serve, combine every 240ml concentrate with 480ml water, or pour over a full glass of ice.

GINGER ORANGEADE

A neighbour taught me how to make this drink as a cold remedy more than twenty years ago. It's a refreshing, invigorating and potent ginger elixir that most definitely clears the cobwebs. Over the years I have added orange peel, rose water and honey to mellow its intensity for everyday drinking, as undiluted it's quite a punch to the palate. While this drink is wonderfully refreshing served over ice, I often warm it up, sweeten it, and give it to my kids when they have the sniffles. Use a vegetable peeler or zester to remove the orange peel to avoid the bitter white pith. **MAKES 1.4 LITRES**

5cm piece fresh ginger, peeled and thinly sliced

Zest of 1 orange

Juice of 8 oranges (navels and Valencias are best)

2 drops of rose water

Honey or sugar for sweetening (optional)

Cinnamon sticks, for serving

Scoop of orange or ginger sorbet, for seving (optional)

Pour 960ml water into a medium saucepan. Add the ginger and orange peel and bring to the boil over a high heat. Reduce the heat to maintain a simmer and simmer for another 15–20 minutes to infuse the flavours. If you have less than 240ml water left in the saucepan, add another 240ml. Add the orange juice and rose water and sweeten with honey or sugar, if desired. Serve warm, garnished with a cinnamon stick, or chilled, with a scoop of orange or ginger sorbet.

SUN-DRIED APRICOT NECTAR

AMARDEEN

Easy on the stomach, full of potassium, and teeming with natural sugars (which provide a healthy energy surge), amardeen is sipped directly after the end of the daily Ramadan fast. It takes its name – and is made from – concentrated apricot fruit leather, which is sold in slabs in Middle Eastern markets (and online). That fruit leather is a product well worth searching for. While I provide alternate ingredients for most recipes, you simply can't replicate this drink with fresh or dried apricots. True amardeen is associated with its robust flavour, silky texture, and smooth consistency, although it certainly wouldn't hurt to garnish it with a few flaked almonds or pine nuts. Amardeen generally needs very little in the way of extra sweetness, but you can add honey or sugar to taste if needed. And feel free to adjust the texture by thinning it out with water or ice if you like. **MAKES 1.4 LITRES**

400g chopped amardeen
960ml boiling water
1.4 litres cold water
1 tablespoon rose water
1 tablespoon orange blossom water

Place the amardeen in a large heatproof bowl and cover it with the boiling water. Drape a tea towel over the top and let the amardeen sit overnight to rehydrate.

Stir the plumped amardeen with a wooden spoon until it becomes a smooth paste. Transfer it to a jug and add the cold water, rose water and orange blossom water. Stir well to combine and chill in the refrigerator before serving.

Amardeen

Consider amardeen the ultimate fruit roll-up. Sold in massive sheets wrapped up in orange cellophane and found widely in Middle Eastern markets, this compressed apricot paste is adored by kids. Snip off a corner for a (relatively) good-for-you snack.

OVERLEAF, FROM LEFT: Sun-Dried Apricot Nectar, Golden Turmeric Milk, Iced Hibiscus Tea, Rose Water Lemonade.

GOLDEN TURMERIC MILK

Turmeric has been used for centuries for its intense flavour and colour as well as its extensive health benefits. Though it has ancient roots, there's no doubt it's the trendy spice of the moment. You'll now find turmeric milk (aka golden milk) in upscale coffee shops and cafés, where they're charging over the odds for this chic 'miracle drink'. But it's easy enough to put together at home. You can make this satisfying drink in big batches and enjoy it as a soothing warm cup in colder weather or over ice in summer. **MAKES 960ML**

960ml almond milk or cow's milk

1 tablespoon vanilla extract, or ½ whole vanilla pod boiled with the milk and scraped

½ tablespoon peeled and finely grated fresh ginger, or 1½ teaspoons ground ginger

5cm piece fresh turmeric roots, peeled and finely grated

½ teaspoon ground turmeric

¼ teaspoon rose water

70g honey or 50g sugar, or to taste

Bring the milk to the boil in a medium saucepan. Add the remaining ingredients, reduce the heat to maintain a simmer and simmer for 3 minutes. Strain and serve.

NOTE: Top your turmeric ginger milk with a few flaked almonds and/or pine nuts for a bit of texture.

ANISE TEA

YANSOUN

Yansoun is an anise tea that is a very common digestif in the Middle East. Similar to chamomile, it settles the stomach, soothes the senses and is the perfect pick-me-up during the dead of winter.

Every time I brew a mug of yansoun, I get flashbacks of my grandmother boiling a huge kettle full of seeds that would fill the house with a distinct liquorice-y, fennel-like aroma. Not only is yansoun caffeine-free, making it an ideal after-dinner or just-before-bed drink, the anise releases a natural sweetness as it cooks so that no sugar, honey or additional flavourings are needed. **MAKES 720ML**

3 tablespoons aniseeds

Combine the aniseeds and 720ml water in a medium saucepan and bring to the boil. Reduce the heat to maintain a simmer and simmer for 5–10 minutes, until the tea turns a dark yellow, almost green colour. Pour through a fine-mesh sieve, discard the anise seeds, and serve.

CINNAMON TEA

AYNAR

This incomparably fragrant, cinnamon-spiked tea traditionally would be served to new mothers right after their babies were born. Sweet and earthy, warming and healing, it's well-known to have a calming effect on the stomach. The most wonderful thing about this drink, though, is the garnish. It's like the icing on a cupcake. The primary ingredient is cinnamon, a pantry staple for most families. But by adding just a handful of nuts – almonds, walnuts and pistachios, or, if you're feeling like a big spender, pine nuts – and perhaps some plumped raisins or shredded coconut, it turns a wintry, everyday drink into something truly special. **MAKES 960ML**

1 tablespoon ground cinnamon
2 cinnamon sticks
½ teaspoon fennel seeds
Brown sugar or honey, for sweetening
Raisins and/or nuts, for serving

Place the ground cinnamon, cinnamon sticks, and fennel seeds in a medium saucepan and add 960ml water. Bring to the boil over a high heat and add 240ml water. Reduce the heat to maintain a simmer and simmer for 30–40 minutes, until the liquid takes on a dark, burnished colour.

Serve in teacups, garnished with the cinnamon sticks and sweetened and garnished as desired (you can leave out the nuts, but in my opinion, the raisins are far from optional!).

NOTE: For stronger tea, let the cinnamon steep longer. For lighter tea, steep them less. You can keep this tea for up to 1 week in the refrigerator and drink it cold or heat it up. You also can add a splash to your oatmeal in the morning or mix it into your coffee to spice it up.

SAGE & FENNEL TEA

Tea is widely consumed in the Middle East, sometimes just for it's flavour and caffein and other times for medicinal and healing purposes. And while undeniably yummy, sage and fennel tea is widely considered to be one of the latter. Although sage is used these days in all manner of roasts, braises and stews, we grew up only knowing sage – or *meramyeh*, as we called it – as tea. A curative, all-powerful wonder tea at that. It was used as a stomach settler and to treat fevers, colds and sore throats, and it was believed to have antimicrobial qualities.

Boiled sage has a tendency to taste a bit bitter (that's how you know it's working!), so you'll want to add a bit of honey, which has been long celebrated for its healing abilities as well. **MAKES 720ML**

1 tablespoon fennel seeds
3 sprigs fresh sage, or 3 tablespoons dried sage
Honey, for sweetening

Combine the fennel seeds, sage and 720ml water in a medium saucepan and bring to the boil over a high heat. Reduce the heat to maintain a simmer and cook for 5–10 minutes, until the tea is fragrant and turns a rich green colour. Strain through a fine-mesh sieve into a teapot, sweeten with honey and serve.

SIPPING CUSTARD
WITH ORANGE BLOSSOM

IMHALABEEYA

When we were teenagers, we thought nothing of taking a winter drive to Jerusalem just so we could get our hands on this ancient sipping pudding during the colder months. It is as much a festive dessert as it is a dressed-up beverage. If you're sensitive to dairy products, this recipe works just as well with nut milks. **MAKES 960ML**

960ml milk
3 tablespoons cornflour
¼ teaspoon mastic
140g honey
1 tablespoon orange blossom water

TOPPINGS
30g chopped pistachios
25g chopped walnuts
2 tablespoons pine nuts (optional)
35g golden raisins

In a medium saucepan, whisk the cornflour into 120ml of the milk. Add the remaining milk to the cornflour slurry, then add the mastic, honey and orange blossom water. Cook over a medium-low heat until the mixture begins to thicken, 10–15 minutes, stirring constantly so it doesn't stick to the bottom of the pan. Remove from the heat and let sit until cool enough to drink (but still nice and hot). Serve in glasses garnished with the nuts and raisins.

WHITE COFFEE

So simple and so soothing! This holds no similarity to a western style milky, caffeine packed white coffee. Instead, this wonderful hot beverage is a digestive and an excellent caffeine-free after-dinner drink which is popular in the Middle East. **MAKES 1 SERVING**

2 tablespoons orange blossom water
Boiling water
Pine nuts (optional)

Pour the orange blossom water into a mug and fill the mug with boiling water. Stir to combine and garnish with pine nuts, if using.

A CULTURAL GUIDE TO HEALING HERBS

Middle Easterners have looked to the curative properties of spices and herbs a lot longer than they've depended on pills. So from za'atar used for a memory boost in the morning, to tea steeped with anise to still your nerves at the end of the day, the following herbs are as beneficial for your body as they are culturally significant and delightful to eat.

ALLSPICE: Actually just one spice, these dried berries can go in a sweet or savoury direction. They're an essential addition to both my Kibbeh and Tanoreen spice blends, but are also used to flavour puddings and pies. Allspice can act as a mild anesthetic as well – considering my arthritis, I may just shake a little seasoning into a warm bath.

CARDAMOM: My mom always opened a couple of pods into the water when she boiled chicken. We generally use cardamom for coffee, although it's also great with tea. The health benefits of cardamom are endless, from improving blood circulation to helping control high cholesterol.

CLOVES: Clove oil has anesthetic properties and can be used to treat toothaches. It doesn't hurt that it's tasty too – in fact, it appears in my signature Tanoreen Spice Mix.

CORIANDER: They are the seeds of coriander, but coriander has an entirely different taste than the polarising green herb. Floral and citrusy when raw and mild and nutty when toasted, coriander is wonderful in rubs and adds tantalising flavour to curry. Its essential oils also help ease irritation, so consider using your spice as a face mask as well!

CUMIN: Research shows that cumin seeds are good for digestion. We add them when cooking beans to counteract stomach bloating. We make kibbeh with it, otherwise the cracked wheat expands in your stomach, and the same goes for falafel.

NIGELLA: Also known as black seed, nigella is mentioned in the Koran for its health-giving qualities. The oil is used for cleaning out the kidneys and liver and is sold in shops throughout the Middle East. Its culinary uses include topping bread and Syrian cheese.

ROSEMARY: It's said that if you stick a stem of rosemary behind your ear, your memory will improve by 50 per cent. My stocker seems to believe it, as he came down the stairs one day practically wearing a wreath! I'd just as soon enjoy it tossed with roasted potatoes, one of the first dishes I enjoyed from a cuisine different from mine.

TURMERIC: Turmeric is thought to help counter so many diseases. I use it as a spice and in supplement form and I believe it has helped keep my arthritis in check.

ZA'ATAR: Za'atar is well-known for improving memory. When we would struggle with our lessons, our third grade Hebrew schoolteacher used to say, 'Oh, you didn't have your za'atar this morning!' No wonder it gets sprinkled on flatbread (page 33) for breakfast.

SAUCES, MARINADES & GLAZES

THE FOUNDATION OF FLAVOUR

Sauces may seem like an afterthought, but they lay the foundation, quite literally, for so many of the dishes in this book. They're an integral part of my kitchen, so when I write about balancing and layering flavours, it always starts with sauces.

Classic Middle Eastern condiments – in particular my All-Purpose Tahini Sauce (page 209) and Hot Pepper Paste (page 212) – have a permanent place with grilled meats and falafel sandwiches, but also provide the building blocks for further experimentation. They set the stage for next-level sauces that are used at Tanoreen by the gallon, as dips, marinades, salad dressings and more.

My lemony Tahini Pomegranate Hot Sauce (page 209) is infinitely adaptable, equally at home drizzled over steaks of deep-fried cauliflower as it is slicked atop raw spicy greens. Consider adding herby Coriander-Basil Pesto (page 216) as a finishing touch for soups just before serving, or use it to infuse flavour into dishes right from the beginning, such as the Walnut-Crusted Fish Fillets (page 160).

And by the way, if you like a certain recipe, make a double, triple or even quadruple batch and freeze whatever you're not using. You'll find your life is so much easier when all you have to do at the end of the day is roast some meat or vegetables and let your ready-to-go sauce do the rest. That's why I call sauces, marinades and glazes part of the 'cold pantry'. They're staple items from which – if you always have them to hand – you can get endless meals with little to no work.

ALL-PURPOSE TAHINI SAUCE

The essential building block of a sauce, this is an almost instant path to houmous (see pages 43 to 44). **MAKES 480ML**

165g tahini
1½ teaspoons chopped garlic
120ml fresh lemon juice
1 teaspoon sea salt

Combine all the ingredients in a blender or food processor, add 120ml water, and blend for 2–3 minutes, until completely smooth and pale white in colour. The sauce will keep, covered in the refrigerator, for up to 2 weeks.

TAHINI-POMEGRANATE HOT SAUCE

MAKES 480ML

480ml All-Purpose Tahini Sauce (see recipe left)
2 tablespoons pomegranate molasses
2 tablespoons hot sauce, homemade (page 213) or shop-bought

In a small bowl, whisk together all the ingredients until smooth. The sauce will keep, covered in the refrigerator, for up to 2 weeks.

PAIR WITH
• Spicy Lamb Egg Rolls (page 47)
• Crispy Cauliflower Steak (page 119)
• Butternut Squash Napoleons (page 130)
• Bitter Greens Salad (page 70)

TAHINI YOGURT SAUCE

MAKES 720ML

480ml All-Purpose Tahini Sauce (see previous recipe)
170g low-fat natural yogurt, homemade (page 94) or shop-bought
4 tablespoons pomegranate molasses

In a medium bowl, whisk together all the ingredients until smooth. The sauce will keep, covered in the refrigerator, for up to 2 weeks.

PAIR WITH
• Everything Grilled Cheese Sandwiches (page 28)
• Fillet Steak Shawarma Sliders (page 57)
• Portobello Shawarma (page 103)
• Stuffed Aubergine over Toasted Pitta (page 109)

TARATOR

MAKES 480ML

480ml All-Purpose Tahini Sauce (page 209)
Zest of ½ lime
25g chopped fresh flat-leaf parsley
Juice of 1 lemon, or more to taste
½ teaspoon diced garlic
½ long hot or jalapeño chilli, diced (optional)

In a small bowl, whisk together the tahini, lime zest
and parsley. Add the lemon juice, garlic and chilli, if
using, and whisk to combine. (This will keep for up to
a week in the refrigerator if you wait to add the parsley
until just before serving.)

PAIR WITH
• Walnut-Crusted Fillet of Fish (page 160)
• Grilled Fish Kebabs (page 162)

Talking About Tahini

While I strive for my food to be as flavourful as
possible, I don't like cluttered food and try to
avoid overloading my pantries. So whether I'm
cooking at home or coming up with new dishes
at the restaurant, my philosophy is simple – go
for versatile ingredients. Every ingredient I use
has to have a specific purpose, and time and
again, I find that tahini fits the bill. Made from
nothing more or less than pure milled sesame
seeds, the luscious paste adds body to sauces
and salad dressings (making it easy to eat
your vegetables), does double-duty as dessert
(pressed into cakes of halawi or combined
with carob molasses or honey to spread on
bread), supplies interesting citrus notes (which
brightens dishes rather than weighing them
down), and contributes a creamy, indulgent
richness without using butter or cream.

In short, tahini is all-in. And it's also in,
making waves well outside the Middle Eastern
kitchen. Though it may be calorically dense,
tahini is considered a 'good fat', heart-healthy,
an excellent source of protein and fibre and full
of essential minerals and vitamins. And just a
small portion of paste can make a large batch of
All-Purpose Tahini Sauce (page 209), a building
block in my cooking that has more uses than
I can count. So make yourself a sizable supply
and keep it to hand in the refrigerator so you
can instantly whip up houmous, whisk with
sesame oil and fresh ginger to make a salad
dressing, dress roasted fish or vegetables,
thicken a curry, assemble sandwiches or even
bake up a batch of cookies. I think you get the
idea. Tahini is the good stuff.

FORTY CLOVES OF GARLIC SAUCE

THOUM

Like the famous forty cloves of garlic chicken dish, this dressing also contains forty cloves of pure raw allium heat and bite. A little goes a long way. Casually called 'white sauce' by some, this sauce is absolutely fantastic on sandwiches (shawarma in particular), spread sparingly on toast to accompany soup and used in marinades. It's also a perfect match for juicy rotisserie chicken.

The ancient Egyptians used raw garlic as an antibiotic and antibacterial, and to this day, my aunt rubs a raw clove on bread with olive oil every morning. Think about how rejuvenated you'll feel after forty cloves! Just make sure you have breath mints close to hand. **MAKES ABOUT 480ML**

40 cloves garlic, peeled

3 tablespoons distilled white vinegar

2 large egg whites

1 teaspoon sea salt

1 teaspoon lemon salt (or sea salt sprinkled with lemon zest)

300ml corn or vegetable oil

Place the garlic in a food processor or blender and process until the cloves are broken up completely. With motor running, slowly stream in the vinegar, egg whites, sea salt and lemon salt through the opening in the lid. Blend until completely incorporated and you can barely see individual specks of garlic. With the motor still running, very slowly stream the oil through the opening in the lid a few drops at a time. This should take between 5 and 10 minutes; that's how slowly the oil should be added. Continue blending until the sauce is thick and silky with the consistency of a rich cream. The sauce will keep in an airtight container in the refrigerator for up to 1 week.

A GARLIC TRICK: Don't relish the thought of peeling forty garlic cloves? Before you grab for a package of peeled garlic, here's a quick trick. Stick the entire head in the microwave for 20 seconds or so and the papery skins will slip right off. The brief blitz of heat can also help tame garlic's pungent bite, leaving you with all the immune-boosting benefits of raw garlic, but without the dragon breath.

PAIR WITH
- Fillet Steak Shawarma Sliders (page 57)
- Portobello Shawarma (page 103)
- Harissa Baked Chicken (page 135)
- Holiday Roasted Leg of Lamb (page 156)

HARISSA

Not just about heat, this next-level chillie paste – omnipresent in North Africa and throughout the Middle East – brings a toasty kick of spice to the party. It's a ready-to-go condiment and makes a great rub for grilled vegetables or roasted meats.

MAKES ABOUT 480ML

60ml olive oil
60g diced poblano chilli
1 tablespoon chopped garlic
½ teaspoon ground caraway
½ teaspoon ground cumin
½ teaspoon freshly ground black pepper
240ml Hot Pepper Paste (see right)
3 tablespoons fresh lemon juice

Heat the oil in a small frying pan or saucepan over a medium heat. Add the chillies and cook until softened, about 3 minutes. Add the garlic and cook until fragrant, about 1 minute. Add the caraway, cumin and black pepper and cook until aromatic, about 1 minute. Add the hot pepper paste and lemon juice and stir to combine. Reduce the heat to maintain a simmer and cook for 2 minutes more, so the flavours combine. Let cool completely, then store in an airtight container in the refrigerator for up to a month.

HOT PEPPER PASTE

A quick glance through this book and you'll find hot pepper paste called for almost as frequently as salt, pepper and olive oil. You're free to buy a jar (which you'll find in the condiment aisle or international section of well-stocked supermarkets, or at any Middle Eastern market). But it's just as easy to make it yourself. That way, you can control the quality (by eschewing preservatives), flavour (selecting smoky peppers, for instance, or avoiding salt), and even the heat (by using milder chillies or removing the seeds and ribs). **MAKES ABOUT 480ML**

170g dried red chillies (I use Aleppo chillies, but any variety will do)
2 tablespoons olive oil, or as needed

Simmer the chillies in a pan of water until fully rehydrated and tender, 10–15 minutes. Transfer the chillies to an ice water bath, drain into a colander and run cold water over them or let them sit until cool enough to handle.

Wearing disposable gloves (very important!), cut the stem ends off the chillies. Slice them lengthways, and use your fingers or a paring knife to scrape away the ribs and seeds (unless you want your paste to be really spicy). Chop the chillies, then put them in a food processor, add the oil and process to a thick paste. The paste will keep, stored in an airtight container in the refrigerator, for at least 1 month.

PAIR WITH
- Green Za'atar Puffs (page 58)
- Cocktail Mushrooms (page 39)
- Halloumi Bites (page 63)
- Kibbeh Cups (page 60)

SPICY TOMATO SAUCE

This is so versatile; you can braise chicken in it, stew beef with it, thin it down with stock or wine to make a base for stew or soups, toss it with sautéed green beans or pasta, cool it down and use it as a chunky tomato salsa, or purée it and spike it for the ultimate brunch-time Bloody Mary! **MAKES ABOUT 2 LITRES**

120ml olive oil
135g diced shallots
1 tablespoon diced garlic
1 poblano or long hot chilli, diced
1½ teaspoons ground cumin
1 tablespoon freshly ground black pepper
1 tablespoon sea salt
1kg diced fresh tomatoes
2 tablespoons Hot Pepper Paste (page 212)
Juice of 1 lemon
400g tinned crushed tomatoes

Heat the oil in a large frying pan over a medium heat. Add the shallots and cook for 3–4 minutes, until softened. Add the garlic and chilli and cook for 2 minutes, or until the garlic is lightly browned. Add the cumin, black pepper and salt and cook for 2 minutes, until aromatic. Add the fresh tomatoes and hot pepper paste and cook, occasionally gently mashing with a fork or spoon, for 8–10 minutes, until the tomatoes begin to break down. Add the lemon juice and crushed tomatoes and bring to the boil. Reduce the heat to maintain a simmer and cook for 5 more minutes. The sauce will keep, stored in an airtight container in the refrigerator, for up to 1 week.

PAIR WITH
- Spinach and Cheese Pastry Triangles (page 26)
- Halloumi Bites (page 63)
- Chicken and Aubergine Rollatini (page 138)

OVERLEAF, FROM LEFT: Hot Pepper Paste, All-Purpose Tahini Sauce, Forty Cloves of Garlic Sauce, Pomegranate-Tamarind Glaze, Cilantro-Basil Pesto.

CORIANDER-BASIL PESTO

I am a staunch believer in coriander. In this pesto it is tempered with fragrant basil and buttery almonds. This pesto is more of a dipping/drizzling/dunking sauce than a pasta topping. It's great as a marinade or a glaze for grilled salmon, it's out of this world tossed with lettuce and tomato over veal or chicken cutlets, and you can enjoy it on its own with warm flatbread dipped into it. My very favourite way to use this pesto is to thin it with lemon juice or olive oil and serve it alongside fried items like Spicy Lamb Egg Rolls (page 47). **MAKES ABOUT 480ML**

25g chopped fresh basil

25g chopped fresh coriander

1 tablespoon chopped garlic

120ml fresh lemon juice

1½ teaspoons freshly ground black pepper

35g grated Parmesan cheese

60g raw flaked almonds

120ml olive oil, or as needed

Combine all the ingredients except the oil in a blender or food processor and pulse until the garlic and almonds are completely broken down. Slowly stream in the oil through the hole in the lid until you have a smooth, perfectly blended sauce that is thick but not pasty. If it's too thick, add a little more oil. The sauce will keep, in an airtight container in the refrigerator, for up to 2 weeks (or indefinitely in the freezer).

PAIR WITH
- Spinach and Cheese Pastry Triangles (page 26)
- Crunchy Kohlrabi & Jicama Slaw (page 77)
- Warm Orzo with Artichoke Hearts (page 86)
- Artichoke & Tomato Sauté with Pesto (page 83)
- Walnut-Crusted Fish Fillets (page 160)

The Art of Emulsification. Emulsification is the all-important process of binding liquids to fat. You know how they say oil and water don't mix? That's also true of oil and vinegar — and my favourite liquid, lemon juice, too. But when you bring an emulsifier such as egg yolk, mustard, hot pepper paste, honey or my beloved tahini to the party, it magically blends the two disparate ingredients together, resulting in a perfectly silky sauce or dressing that only requires a quick whisk.

TEKLAI

Almost by definition, soups and stews consist
of ingredients that slowly combine together to
become a delectable — yet sometimes rather
one-note — whole. That's where this quick sauté
of olive oil infused with garlic and coriander
comes in. Drizzled over the top at the last
second, it provides a contrasting element that
is nothing less than intoxicating. This is my most
faithful take on a classic teklai, although you'll
find other variations elsewhere in this book
including one that incorporates fresh coriander
(pictured right, see pages 90 and 126) and one
enriched with almonds (see page 145).

MAKES 240ML

120ml olive oil
20 cloves garlic, finely chopped
1½ teaspoons sea salt
1½ teaspoons freshly ground black pepper
15g ground coriander

Heat the oil in a small frying pan over a medium heat.
Add the garlic and cook until softened and fragrant,
about 3 minutes. Add the salt, pepper and coriander
and cook until the mixture is aromatic and the garlic
is golden brown, about 3 minutes. Remove from the
heat and use immediately, or cool, transfer to an
airtight container and store in the refrigerator, where
it will keep for up to 1 week.

TANOREEN PEANUT SAUCE

We have all come to know and love savoury, nutty peanut sauce as a traditional condiment used in South Asian cooking. And by now, you also know I enjoy bucking tradition.

I first came across this lip-smacker when I went back to finish university in my forties. I scouted out the best local restaurants so I could sneak off for lunch between classes. I found a gem called ASIA on Lexington Avenue in Manhattan, and one of my favourite discoveries was their chicken satay paired with a gingery, faintly spicy peanut sauce. It wasn't lost on me that chicken satay is basically the Indonesian/Thai equivalent of Middle Eastern chicken kebabs. The wheels in my head were turning.

I thought of my daughter, who loves peanut butter so much she used to eat it out of the jar with a spoon. I swapped some of the peanut butter for tahini, added Coriander-Basil Pesto, and drizzled in some pomegranate molasses to highlight the sweet and sour nature of the sauce. Initially I re-created this satay sauce for my daughter as a dipper for chicken wings, but now we all love my version with my Spicy Lamb Egg Rolls (page 47). **MAKES 720ML**

1 tablespoon chopped garlic

1 poblano chilli, diced

1 tablespoon diced fresh lemongrass

½ teaspoon grated fresh ginger

25g fresh Thai basil leaves

120ml rice vinegar

120ml fresh lemon juice

120ml soy sauce

4 tablespoons smooth peanut butter

3 tablespoons tahini

2 tablespoons pomegranate molasses

2 tablespoons tamarind paste

1 tablespoon Coriander-Basil Pesto (page 216) or shop-bought pesto

1 tablespoon chilli oil

2 tablespoons sesame oil

Combine the garlic, chilli, lemongrass, ginger and basil in a food processor and pulse until completely broken down. Add the vinegar, lemon juice and soy sauce and pulse until combined. Add the peanut butter, tahini, pomegranate molasses, tamarind paste and pesto and pulse until the mixture forms a paste. Slowly drizzle in the chilli oil and sesame oil through the hole in the lid and process until it becomes a sauce, adding a touch of water, if needed, to reach your desired consistency. The sauce will keep, covered in the refrigerator, for up to 1 week.

PAIR WITH
- Spicy Lamb Egg Rolls (page 47)
- Grilled Sesame Prawns (page 168)

POMEGRANATE-TAMARIND GLAZE

This sweet and sour flavour bomb is as delicious over roasted vegetables as it is alongside a thick steak or lamb kebabs. Make a big batch and freeze it in ice cube trays so you can pop them out and use them at will. **MAKES 480ML**

4 tablespoons olive oil

2 shallots, finely diced

1 long hot or poblano chilli, finely diced (optional)

1 tablespoon finely diced garlic

½ teaspoon ground cumin

1 teaspoon freshly ground black pepper

1 tablespoon ground turmeric

Sea salt

960ml unsweetened pomegranate juice

240ml fresh orange juice

480ml tomato juice

240ml tamarind paste concentrate

3 tablespoons grape molasses

Heat the oil in a medium saucepan over a medium heat. Add the shallots and chilli, if using, and cook until softened, 3–5 minutes. Add the garlic and cook until fragrant, about 2 minutes. Add the cumin, black pepper and turmeric, season with salt and cook until aromatic, about 2 minutes. Add the pomegranate juice, orange juice, tomato juice, tamarind, and grape molasses and bring to the boil. Reduce the heat to maintain a simmer and simmer, stirring occasionally, for 30–40 minutes, until the sauce reduces by two-thirds. The sauce will keep, in an airtight container in the refrigerator, for up to 1 week.

PAIR WITH

• Freekeh-Stuffed Turnips (page 112)
• Aleppo-Style Kibbeh Stew (page 146)
• Sweet & Spicy Braised Beef Rolls (page 151)

SEAFOOD MARINADE

Want a one-pan dinner? Pour this fail-safe blend over a side of vegetables such as baby onions, halved baby potatoes, carrots or cauliflower and roast in the oven or grill them alongside your fish or seafood. **MAKES 480ML**

2 plum tomatoes, peeled, seeded, and grated on a box grater

15g chopped fresh coriander

4 cloves garlic, finely diced

15g chopped fresh basil leaves

5–6 fresh sage leaves, finely chopped

3 tablespoons chopped fresh dill, or 1 tablespoon dill seeds, toasted and crushed

1 tablespoon Hot Pepper Paste (page 212)

1 tablespoon ground cumin

1 tablespoon freshly ground black pepper

1 tablespoon ground coriander

Juice of 2 lemons

120ml olive oil

Combine all the ingredients in a large nonreactive bowl (such as stainless steel) and whisk until emulsified. The marinade will keep in an airtight container in the refrigerator for up to 1 week.

PAIR WITH

• Pan-Roasted Salmon (page 159)
• Grilled Fish Kebabs (page 162)

INDEX

aubergine, 110
  & Chicken Rollatini,
    138–40, 139
  Hash with Tomatoes, 87
  Honey-Cured, 182, 183
  Stuffed, over Toasted
    Pita, 108, 109–10
ackawi, 50
Aleppo-Style Kibbeh Stew
  with Carrots, 146–48,
  147
allspice, 205
almond:
  ground, 13
  Paste, 187
  Teklai, 145
  Triple, Cake, 186, 187
Amardeen, 199, 200
Anise Tea, 202
Apricot, Sun-Dried,
  Nectar, 199, 200
artichoke(s):
  Christmas Seafood, 170,
    171–72, 173
  Hearts, Warm Orzo
    with, 86
  how to prepare, 172
  & Tomato Sauté with
    Pesto, 83
asparagus:
  Casserole, Spring, 23
  Four Cheese Frittata, 19
avocado:
  Houmous, 44, 45
  Smashed Broad Beans
    with, 22
Aynar, 203

Bahraini Chicken with
  Rice, 141
Baklava, Chocolate, 178,
  179
Basil-Coriander Pesto,
  216, 215
basmati rice, 13

Batata Harrah, 91
beef:
  Aleppo-Style Kibbeh
    Stew with Carrots,
    146–48, 147
  Braised Oxtails with
    Olives, 155
  Fillet Steak Shawarma
    Sliders, 56, 57
  & Mushroom Stew with
    Almond Teklai, 145
  Rolls, Sweet & Sour, 150,
    151
  Stew with Quince, 154
beet:
  greens, 71
  Roasted, Houmous,
    43, 45
Bitter Greens with Sweet
  Tahini Dressing, 70
black pepper, 13
Bourekas, 26
broad beans:
  Fresh, with Spiced
    Yogurt Sauce, 115
  Smashed, with Avocado,
    22
bulgur, 13
  see also kibbeh
Butter Cookie Sandwiches,
  192, 193
butternut squash:
  Houmous, 43, 45
  Napoleons, 130, 131
  Olive Oil, & Carrot Cake,
    177

cabbage:
  Rawia's Sweet & Sour
    Soup, 125
  red, in Autumn
    Fattoush, 78, 79
cakes:
  Jam & Tahini Squares,
    180

Olive Oil, Butternut
  Squash, & Carrot, 177
Triple Almond, 186, 187
Caraway Pudding with
  Nuts & Honey, 188
Carawia, 188
cardamom, 205
cauliflower:
  Steaks, Crispy,
    with Tahini &
    Pomegranate, 118,
    119
  Tahini Tajine, 111
cheese(s):
  Arabic, 50
  Four, Frittata, 19
  Sandwiches, Everything
    Grilled, 28, 29
  & Spinach Pastry
    Triangles, 26
  String, Syrian, 48, 49
  & Sujok (for
    manakeesh), 34, 35
  see also halloumi;
    kashkaval
chicken:
  Curry, Tahini, 132
  & Aubergine Rollatini,
    138–40, 139
  Five Onion, 133
  Harissa Baked, 134, 135
  Kibbeh, Baked, 136, 137
  with Rice, Bahraini, 141
chickpea(s), 13
  Soup with Pearl Onions,
    121
  Squash with, in Minted
    Yogurt, 92, 93
  see also houmous
chicory, 71
  Bitter Greens with Sweet
    Tahini Dressing, 70
chillies, 54
  dried, 13
  Hot Pepper Paste, 212,
    214

Oil-Cured, with Walnut
  Stuffing, 52, 53, 55
chocolate:
  Baklava, 178, 179
  -Dipped & Pistachio-
    Stuffed Fruit, 181
Christmas Seafood
  Artichokes, 170,
    171–72, 173
Cinnamon Tea, 203
cloves, 205
Cocktail Mushrooms with
  Three Cheeses, 39
Compote, Stone Fruit, 185
condiments:
  Almond Teklai, 145
  Harissa, 213
  hot chile oil, 13
  hot pepper paste, 14,
    212, 214
  Teklai, 126, 217
Cookie, Butter,
  Sandwiches, 192, 193
coriander:
  Basil Pesto, 216, 215
  Salata, 67
coriander, 205
  Green Beans with
    Toasted Almonds,
    96, 97
cumin, 205
Curry, Tahini Chicken, 132
custard:
  & Nut Crumble, Layered,
    190, 191
  Sipping, with Orange
    Blossom, 204

dandelion greens, 71
  Bitter Greens with Sweet
    Tahini Dressing, 70
Dukkah-Spiced Lentil
  Spread, 46

Egg Rolls, Spicy Lamb, 47
eggs:
    Falafel Scotch, 24, 25
    Four Cheese Frittata, 19
    Green Tomato
        Shakshuka, 20, 21
    Rolled Mushroom
        Omelettes, 27
    Spring Asparagus
        Casserole, 23
Egyptian-Style Lentil &
    Noodle Pilaf, 116–17
Everything Grilled Cheese
    Sandwiches, 28, 29
An Excuse for Kibbeh,
    104–7, 105, 106

Falafel Scotch Eggs, 24, 25
Fattoush, Autumn, 78, 79
fennel:
    Freekeh Salad with
        Spring Vegetables,
        74, 75
    Pomegranate, & Sage
        Salad, 68, 69
    & Sage Tea, 203
Fillet Steak Shawarma
    Sliders, 56, 57
fish and seafood:
    Aunt Um Sami's Baked
        Fish Kibbeh, 166–67
    Christmas Seafood
        Artichokes, 170,
        171–72, 173
    fish substitutions, 161
    Grilled Fish Kebabs, 162,
        163
    Grilled Sesame Prawns,
        168, 169
    Moroccan-Style Stuffed
        Sardines, 164, 165
    Pan-Roasted Salmon
        with Salsa Khadra,
        158, 159
    Seafood Marinade, 219
    Walnut-Crusted Fish

Fillets, 160
Five Onion Chicken, 133
flatbreads (manakeesh),
    30–34, 35
    Basic, 32, 33
    Gluten-Free, 31
    toppings for, 34
Forty Cloves of Garlic
    Sauce, 211, 215
Four Cheese Frittata, 19
freekeh, 13
    Salad with Spring
        Vegetables, 74, 75
    & Shiitake Soup, 128,
        129
    -Stuffed Turnips with
        Tamarind Sauce,
        112–14, 113
Frittata, Four Cheese, 19

Garlic, Forty Cloves of,
    Sauce, 211, 215
Ginger Orangeade, 198
Glaze, Pomegranate-
    Tamarind, 219, 215
Gluten-Free Flatbread, 31
Goat's Cheese, Tangy
    Roasted Root
    Vegetables with,
    88, 89
Golden Turmeric Milk,
    202, 200
grape molasses, 14
Graybeh, 192, 193
Green Beans, Coriander,
    with Toasted
    Almonds, 96, 97
Green Tomato Shakshuka,
    20, 21
green za'atar (leaves), 59
    Puffs, 58–59
    Watermelon, &
        Halloumi Salad, 72,
        73
grilled:
    Cheese Sandwiches,

Everything, 28, 29
    Sweetcorn Salad, 82
    Fish Kebabs, 162, 163
    Sesame Prawns, 168,
        169

halloumi, 50
    Bites with Hot Tomato
        Jam, 62, 63
    Cocktail Mushrooms
        with Three Cheeses,
        39
    Everything Grilled
        Cheese Sandwiches,
        28, 29
    Four Cheese Frittata, 19
    Green Za'atar Puffs,
        58–59
    Watermelon, & Za'atar
        Salad, 72, 73
Harissa, 213
    Baked Chicken, 134,
        135
healing herbs, 205
Hibiscus Tea, Iced, 197,
    201
Holiday Roasted Leg of
    Lamb, 156, 157
Honey-Cured Aubergine,
    182, 183
hot chillie oil, 13
hot pepper paste, 14, 212,
    214
Hot Sauce, 116, 117
    Tahini-Pomegranate,
        209
Hot Tomato Jam, 62, 63
houmous, 42–44
    Avocado, 44, 45
    Butternut Squash, 43, 45
    Roasted Beetroot, 43, 45
    Roasted Pepper, 44, 45

Iced Hibiscus Tea, 197, 201
Iijeh, 27

Imhalabeeya, 204

Jam & Tahini Squares, 180
Jerusalem artichokes, 120
    & Sage Sauté, 120
    & Sweet Potato Soup,
        126, 127
jibneh arabieh, 50
jicama, 67
    & Kohlrabi Slaw,
        Crunchy, 76, 77

kale, 71
Karkadeh, 197
kashkaval, 50
    Cocktail Mushrooms
        with Three Cheeses,
        39
    Four Cheese Frittata, 19
Katayef, 189
kebabs, 157
    Grilled Fish, 162, 163
Khabsah, 184
kibbeh, 124, 157
    Chicken, Baked, 136,
        137
    Cups, 60, 61
    An Excuse for, 104–7,
        105, 106
    Fish, Aunt Um Sami's
        Baked, 166–67
    spices, 14
    Stew with Carrots,
        Aleppo-Style, 146–48,
        147
kohlrabi, 67
    Grilled Sweetcorn Salad,
        82
    & Jicama Slaw, Crunchy,
        76, 77
    Tangy Roasted Root
        Vegetables with Goat
        Cheese, 88, 89
Koshari, 116–17
Kshtaleia, 190, 191

labneh, 50
  Red Onions, &
    Kalamata Olives (for
    manakeesh), 34, 35
lamb:
  Egg Rolls, Spicy, 47
  Holiday Roasted Leg
    of, 156
  Kibbeh Cups, 60, 61
  leg of, options for, 157
  -Stuffed Potatoes in
    Tamarind Sauce, 149
  Layered Custard & Nut
    Crumble, 190, 191
  Lebanese Spicy Pan-Fried
    Potatoes, 91
  Leeks, Pan-Roasted
    Potatoes &, with
    Teklai, 90
Lemonade, Rose Water,
    197, 201
lentil(s), 14
  An Excuse for Kibbeh,
    104–7, 105, 106
  & Noodle Pilaf,
    Egyptian-Style,
    116–17
  Spread, Dukkah-Spiced,
    46
limu, 14

Mabroosheh, 180
Machbous, 141
mashi, 148
mahlab, 31
Makdous, 52, 53, 55
Makdous Fetti, 108,
    109–10
manakeesh, see flatbreads
mastic, 14
Milk, Golden Turmeric,
    202, 200
Molasses Pudding,
    Swirled, 184
Moroccan-Style Stuffed
    Sardines, 164, 165
mushroom(s):
  Beef &, Stew with
    Almond Teklai, 145

Cocktail, with Three
    Cheeses, 39
  Omelettes, Rolled, 27
  Portobello Shawarma,
    103
  Shiitake & Freekeh Soup,
    128, 129
mustard greens, 71

nabulsi, 50
Na'ir, 98
Napoleons, Butternut
    Squash, 130, 131
nigella, 205
noodle:
  & Lentil Pilaf, Egyptian-
    Style, 116–17
  Vermicelli & Rice Pilaf,
    140
nut(s), 14
  Chocolate Baklava, 178,
    179
  Layered Custard &,
    Crumble, 190, 191

Oil-Cured Chiles with
    Walnut Stuffing, 52,
    53, 55
olive oil, 14, 19, 144
  Butternut Squash, &
    Carrot Cake, 177
Omelettes, Rolled
    Mushroom, 27
onion(s):
  Five, Chicken, 133
  Pearl, Chickpea Soup
    with, 121
Orangeade, Ginger, 198
orange blossom (water),
    14
  Sipping Custard with,
    204
  White Coffee, 204
Orzo with Artichoke
    Hearts, Warm, 86
Oxtails, Braised, with
    Olives, 155

panko, 14
parsley:
  Quinoa Tabouleh, 80, 81
  Tarator, 210
pastry:
  Chocolate Baklava, 178,
    179
  Green Za'atar Puffs,
    58–59
  Spinach & Cheese
    Triangles, 26
  Peanut Sauce, Tanoreen,
    218
pepper(s), 54
  Roasted, Houmous,
    44, 45
  see also chiles
Pesto, Coriander-Basil,
    216, 215
pilafs:
  Lentil & Noodle,
    Egyptian-Style,
    116–17
  Quinoa, with Roasted
    Vegetables, 84, 85
  Rice & Vermicelli, 140
Pistachio-Stuffed &
    Chocolate-Dipped
    Fruit, 181
pita chips, in Autumn
    Fattoush, 78, 79
pomegranate:
  Fennel, & Sage Salad,
    68, 69
  how to juice, 152, 153
  molasses, 14, 152
  Tahini Hot Sauce, 209
  Tamarind Glaze, 219,
    215
Portobello Shawarma, 103
potatoes:
  Lamb-Stuffed, in
    Tamarind Sauce, 149
  Lebanese Spicy Pan-
    Fried, 91
  Pan-Roasted Leeks &,
    with Teklai, 90
Poussin, Tanoreen Spiced,
    142, 143–44

Prawns, Grilled Sesame,
    168, 169
puddings:
  Caraway, with Nuts &
    Honey, 188
  Swirled Molasses, 184
  Pumpkin Kibbie, Baked,
    122–24, 123

quince, 185
  Beef Stew with, 154
quinoa, 14
  Pilaf with Roasted
    Vegetables, 84, 85
  -Stuffed Tomatoes,
    40, 41
  Tabouleh, 80, 81

radicchio, in Autumn
    Fattoush, 78, 79
rice:
  Bahraini Chicken with,
    141
  basmati, 13
  Spicy Skillet-Crusted, 95
  & Vermicelli Pilaf, 140
  Rollatini, Chicken &
    Aubergine, 138–40,
    139
  Rolled Mushroom
    Omelettes, 27
  Root Vegetables, Tangy
    Roasted, with Goat's
    Cheese, 88, 89
rosemary, 205
rose water, 14
  Lemonade, 197, 201

Sage & Fennel Tea, 203
salads, 65–82
  Autumn Fattoush, 78, 79
  Bitter Greens with Sweet
    Tahini Dressing, 70
  Coriander Salata, 67
  Crunchy Kohlrabi &
    Jicama Slaw, 76, 77
  Fennel, Pomegranate, &

Sage, 68, 69
Freekeh, with Spring
    Vegetables, 74, 75
greens for, 71
Grilled Sweetcorn, 82
Quinoa Tabouleh, 80, 81
Watermelon, Halloumi,
    & Za'atar, 72, 73
Salmon, Pan-Roasted,
    with Salsa Khadra,
    158, 159
Salsa Khadra, 159
Sardines, Moroccan-Style
    Stuffed, 164, 165
sauces:
    Coriander-Basil Pesto,
        216, 215
    Garlic, Forty Cloves of,
        211, 215
    Hot, 116, 117
    Hot, Tahini
        Pomegranate, 209
    Hot Tomato Jam, 62, 63
    Peanut, Tanoreen, 218
    Pomegranate-Tamarind
        Glaze, 219, 215
    Tahini, 111
    Tahini, All-Purpose, 209,
        214
    Tahini Yogurt, 209
    Tamarind, 112
    Tarator, 210
    Tomato, Spicy, 213
    Yogurt, Spiced, 115
Scotch Eggs, Falafel, 24, 25
seafood, see fish and
    seafood
Seafood Marinade, 219
Shakshuka, Green Tomato,
    20, 21
shanklish, 50
Sharab, 198
shawarma, 157
    Fillet Steak , Sliders,
        56, 57
    Portobello, 103
    Shiitake & Freekeh Soup,
        128, 129
Shulbato, 84, 85
Sliders, Fillet Steak

Shawarma, 56, 57
soups:
    Chickpea, with Pearl
        Onions, 121
    Freekeh & Shiitake, 128,
        129
    Jerusalem Artichoke &
        Sweet Potato, 126,
        127
    Sweet & Sour, Rawia's,
        125
spice mix, Tanoreen, 15
spinach, 71
    Baked Pumpkin Kibbie,
        122–24, 123
    & Cheese Pastry
        Triangles, 26
    Four Cheese Frittata, 19
    Spring Asparagus
        Casserole, 23
    Spring Vegetables,
        Freekeh Salad with,
        74, 75
squash:
    with Chickpeas in
        Minted Yogurt, 92, 93
    Grilled Sweetcorn Salad,
        82
    Pumpkin Kibbeh, Baked,
        122–24, 123
    Stuffed Aubergine over
        Toasted Pita, 108,
        109–10
    see also butternut
        squash; zucchini
Stone Fruit Compote, 185
string cheese, 50
    Syrian, 48, 49
Sujok & Cheese (for
    manakeesh), 34, 35
sumac, 15
sunchokes, see Jerusalem
    artichoke(s)
Sweetcorn, Grilled, Salad,
    82
Sweet & Sour Beef Rolls,
    150, 151
Sweet & Sour Soup,
    Rawia's, 125
Sweet Potato & Jerusalem

Artichoke Soup, 126,
    127
Swirled Molasses
    Pudding, 184
Swiss chard, 71
Syrian String Cheese,
    48, 49

Tabouleh, Quinoa, 80, 81
tahini, 15, 210
    Chicken Curry, 132
    & Jam Squares, 180
    Pomegranate Hot Sauce,
        209
    Sauce, 111
    Sauce, All-Purpose, 209
    Yogurt Sauce, 209
Tajine, Cauliflower Tahini,
    111
tamarind, 15, 114
    Cooler, 198
    Pomegranate Glaze,
        219, 215
    Sauce, 112
Tarator, 210
teas:
    Anise, 202
    Cinnamon, 203
    Iced Hibiscus, 197, 201
    Sage & Fennel, 203
Teklai, 126, 217
    Almond, 145
Thoum, 211
tomato(es):
    Aubergine Hash with, 87
    & Artichoke Sauté with
        Pesto, 83
    Green, Shakshuka, 20,
        21
    how to peel, 87
    Jam, Hot, 62, 63
    Quinoa-Stuffed, 40, 41
    Sauce, Spicy, 213
    Triple Almond Cake, 186,
        187
turmeric, 205
    Milk, Golden, 202, 200
turnips:
    Freekeh-Stuffed, with
        Tamarind Sauce,

112–14, 113
Tangy Roasted Root
    Vegetables with
    Goat's Cheese, 88, 89

Vermicelli & Rice Pilaf,
    140
vinegar, 15

walnut:
    -Crusted Fish Fillets, 160
    -Stuffed Crescents,
        Crispy, 189
    Stuffing, Oil-Cured
        Chillies with, 52,
        53, 55
watercress, 71
    Bitter Greens with Sweet
        Tahini Dressing, 70
Watermelon, Halloumi, &
    Za'atar Salad, 72, 73
White Coffee, 204

Yansoun, 202
yogurt:
    Homemade, 94
    Minted, Squash with
        Chickpeas in, 92, 93
    Sauce, Spiced, 115
    Tahini Sauce, 209

za'atar, 15, 59, 205
    see also green za'atar
        (leaves)
zucchini:
    Sautéed Hearts of, 98
    Squash with Chickpeas
        in Minted Yogurt,
        92, 93
    Stuffed Aubergine over
        Toasted Pita, 108,
        109–10

Acknowledgments

I want to first acknowledge my parents, who taught me how to cook with love and care. It started there.

To my husband, Wafa: The man who's been with me in constant companionship for more than forty years. My partner in life and my best friend through every up and down. Thank you, my love, for your constant advice, support and passion. I wouldn't want to be on this journey with anyone else.

To my daughter, Jumana: I wish every mother felt lucky enough to have a daughter and best friend she trusts to be her business partner. Your strength of character is matched only by your appreciation of good food, which makes you my first tester when I create a new recipe. Your partnership has helped this business grow and thrive, not just for us, but for a continuity of culture and family.

To my son, Tarek: This is the second book we have worked on together and I wouldn't have it any other way. You are the artist in our family and a superb cook in your own right. Your input and knowledge of food have been invaluable to this book. You helped turn my thoughts and ideas into stories. We share a food philosophy. I smile when I think about your bringing my morning coffee if only to get a story out of me. You light up my life and I thank you with all my heart for all your hard work on this book.

To my staff at Tanoreen: My professional family. The many years we have spent together in the kitchen has helped bring these recipes to life in so many capacities.

To our guests at Tanoreen: These recipes were created in part as a direct result of your tastes, needs and feedback. You have been inspirational and without you, our restaurant wouldn't have been a success.

To my brothers and sisters, family and best friends who have stood with me every step of the way: For the laughs and opinions that matter the most, I thank you.

To team Levant: My writer, Sarah, for being patient, insightful, and genuinely invested in our long afternoons of eating, talking, writing and recipe testing. I wish you continued success. My agent, Judith, for continued direction, support, and encouragement. To our photographer, Con Poulos, and stylist, Simon Andrews: It was a pleasure working with you both. You are artists who were open to suggestions and my ideas, and I thank you for helping create what I think is a beautiful book. Our designer, Jan, for creating a beautiful look for these pages.

Finally to my publisher, Kyle, for believing in me enough to want to publish another book! You understood what I wanted to say with this second book and gave me the space to do it. And to our editor, Chris: You've brought this book to the finish line with finesse and were always there to guide me when I needed it.

An Hachette UK Company
www.hachette.co.uk

First published in Great Britain in 2018 by
Kyle Books, an imprint of Kyle Cathie Ltd
Carmelite House
50 Victoria Embankment
London EC4Y 0DZ
www.kylebooks.co.uk

ISBN 978-0-85783-417-1

Project Editor: Christopher Steighner
Copy Editor: Leda Scheintaub
Designer: Jan Derevjanik
Photographer: Con Poulos
Food Stylist: Simon Andrews
Production: Nic Jones, Gemma John, and Lisa Pinnell

A Cataloguing in Publication record for this title is available from the British Library.

Printed in China

10 9 8 7 6 5 4 3 2 1